CW01086319

face2face

Elementary Student's Book **A**

Chris Redston & Gillie Cunningham

CAMBRIDGE
UNIVERSITY PRESS

Contents

Speaking	Listening and Video	Reading	Writing
Introducing yourself What's your first name? Saying goodbye	Conversations in a classroom First names and surnames		
Names and countries	At the conference	At the conference	
Phone numbers and jobs The conference list	Phone numbers What do you do?	Three conversations	Sentences about you
Numbers Hiring a car	**Help with Listening** Sentence stress (1) VIDEO ▶ Hiring a car	Personal information	Filling in a form
Things in the classroom			
HELP WITH PRONUNCIATION Word stress and syllables p15		**Reading and Writing Portfolio 1 At the hotel** Workbook p64	
Personal possessions	What's important to me? A survey in a shop	What's important to me?	My friend's possessions
My family	Family photos **Help with Listening** Sentence stress (2)	The Brown family	Questions with *How many ... ?*
Buying tickets	What time is it? Times and prices VIDEO ▶ At the cinema	Adverts for an exhibition and for a cinema	
Whose mobile phone is this? Where's Robbie's bag?	Where's the baby?		Sentences with prepositions
HELP WITH PRONUNCIATION The schwa /ə/ in words p23		**Reading and Writing Portfolio 2 My favorite thing** Workbook p66	
Daily routines		Behind the camera	My daily routine Questions about routines
Free time activities Find two people	The office party **Help with Listening** Weak forms (1): *do you ... ?*		Questions with *Do you ... ?*
My important dates What shall we get her?	What's the date today? VIDEO ▶ A birthday present		Dates A conversation
My habits	Early bird or night owl?	Early bird or night owl?	
HELP WITH PRONUNCIATION How we say *th* p31		**Reading and Writing Portfolio 3 All about me** Workbook p68	
My free time activities My partner's free time	Life at the observatory **Help with Listening** Linking (1)		Questions with *Do you ... ?*
Things I like and don't like I've got a friend for you!	First Date!	First Date! Mark's first date	Questions with *Does he/she ... ?*
My favourite café Ordering food and drink	**Help with Listening** Would you like ... ? VIDEO ▶ At the Sun Café	A café menu Conversations in a café	A conversation in a café
Breakfasts around the world My perfect breakfast	What's for breakfast?		
HELP WITH PRONUNCIATION /ʃ/, /tʃ/ and /dʒ/ p39		**Reading and Writing Portfolio 4 Going out** Workbook p70	
When was he born? When I was thirteen	Albert's thirteenth birthday **Help with Listening** Weak forms (2): *was* and *were*	My birthday party	Questions with *was* and *were*
Questions about the past My timeline	**Help with Listening** Present Simple or Past Simple	Cameron's world	
What I did last weekend Asking follow-up questions	VIDEO ▶ How was your weekend?	Four weekends	Writing notes about the past
Too expensive or quite cheap?		Winners and losers	
HELP WITH PRONUNCIATION The letter *o* p47		**Reading and Writing Portfolio 5 A night to remember** Workbook p72	
My internet Find someone who ...	Planet Google	The Google guys	Negative Past Simple sentences Past Simple *yes/no* questions
My mobile, computer and TV	**Help with Listening** *can* and *can't*	Our first colour TV The first mobile phones	My first mobile
Telling news stories	Here is the news VIDEO ▶ Talking about the news **Help with Listening** Sentence stress (3)	Two news reports	
Video games	The father of video games	Shigeru Miyamoto fact file	
HELP WITH PRONUNCIATION Past Simple of regular verbs p55		**Reading and Writing Portfolio 6 Text me!** Workbook p74	

Phonemic Symbols p161   **Irregular Verb List p161**   **Self-study DVD-ROM Instructions p168**

Welcome!

Vocabulary numbers 0–20; the alphabet; things in the classroom; days of the week
Real World introducing yourself; classroom instructions; names; saying goodbye

Hello!

1 **a** `CD1 1` Look at conversation 1 and listen.

b Practise conversation 1 with your teacher. Use your name.

2 **a** `CD1 2` Look at conversation 2 and listen.

b Practise conversation 2 with four students. Use your name.

Numbers 0–20

3 **a** Work in pairs. How do we say these numbers?

0 1 2 3 4 5
6 7 8 9 10
11 12 13 14 15
16 17 18 19 20

b `CD1 3` `PRONUNCIATION` Listen and check. Listen again and practise.

c Work in the same pairs. Say five numbers. Write your partner's numbers. Are they correct?

Classroom instructions

4 **a** Work in new pairs. Which of these instructions do you understand? Check in Language Summary Welcome `REAL WORLD 0.2` p127.

Open your book.
Look at the photo on page 11.
Do exercise 6 on your own.
Look at the board.
Work in pairs.
Work in groups.
Fill in the gaps.
Compare answers.
Listen and check.
Listen and practise.
Match the words to the pictures.
Ask and answer the questions.

b `CD1 4` Listen and tick (✓) the instructions when you hear them.

1
TEACHER Hello. What's your name, please?
DENIZ My name's Deniz Aslan.
TEACHER I'm Peter Adams. Welcome to the class.
DENIZ Thank you.

2
HASSAN Hello, my name's Hassan.
OLGA Hi, I'm Olga.
HASSAN Nice to meet you.
OLGA You too.

The alphabet

5 **a** `CD1 5` `PRONUNCIATION` Listen and practise the alphabet.

Aa Bb Cc Dd Ee Ff Gg Hh Ii
Jj Kk Ll Mm Nn Oo Pp Qq Rr
Ss Tt Uu Vv Ww Xx Yy Zz

b `CD1 6` Listen and write the words.

TIP • ss = *double s*

3
MARCOS Hello. Sorry I'm late.
TEACHER No problem.

Things in the classroom

8 **a** Match these words to pictures a–j.

a table *b*   a chair   a book   a pencil
a pen   a dictionary   a CD player
a TV   a DVD player   a computer

b Work in pairs. Test your partner.

What's picture e?   It's a chair.

Goodbye!

9 **a** Put the days of the week in order.

Friday   Tuesday   Thursday   Monday *1*
Wednesday   Saturday   Sunday

b CD1 10 PRONUNCIATION Listen and check.
Listen again and practise. What day is it today?
What day is it tomorrow?

10 CD1 11 Listen and write the day. Then
practise with other students.

MARCOS Bye, Olga.
OLGA Goodbye. See you on _____ .
MARCOS Yes, see you.

First names and surnames

6 **a** Look at conversation 3. Then match the teacher's
questions 1–3 to Marcos's answers a–c.

1 What's your first name?   a F–U–E–N–T–E–S.
2 What's your surname?   b Fuentes.
3 How do you spell that?   c It's Marcos.

b CD1 7 Listen and check.

c CD1 8 Listen to two conversations, A and B.
Write the names.

7 **a** CD1 9 PRONUNCIATION Listen and practise the
questions in **6a**.

b Ask four students these questions and write
the names.

Progress Portfolio Welcome!

Tick (✓) the things you can do in English.

☐ I can say hello, introduce myself and
say goodbye.

☐ I can say numbers 0–20.

☐ I can understand classroom instructions.

☐ I can say the alphabet.

☐ I can spell my name.

☐ I can say the days of the week.

1A ▶ # How are you?

Vocabulary countries and nationalities
Grammar *be* (1): positive and *Wh-* questions;
subject pronouns and possessive adjectives
Real World introducing people

Listening and Speaking

1 **a** CD1 12 PRONUNCIATION Read and listen to conversation 1. Listen again and practise.

b Practise conversation 1 with four students. Use your name.

2 **a** CD1 13 PRONUNCIATION Read and listen to conversation 2. Listen again and practise.

b Work in groups. Take turns to introduce students to each other.

Vocabulary and Speaking
Countries and nationalities

3 **a** Tick (✓) the countries you know.

countries I'm from …	nationalities I'm …
Brazil	Brazili *a n*
Australia	Australi _ _
Argentina	Argentini _ _
the USA	Americ _ _
Germany	Germ _ _
Italy	Itali _ _
Mexico	Mexic _ _
Russia	Russi _ _
Egypt	Egypti _ _
the UK	Brit *i s h*
Spain	Span _ _
Poland	Pol _ _ _
Turkey	Turk _ _
China	Chin *e s e*
Japan	Japan _ _
France	French

b Write the missing letters in the nationalities. Check in Language Summary 1 **VOCABULARY 1.1** p128.

c Where are you from? What's your nationality?

I'm from Colombia. I'm Korean.

4 **a** CD1 14 Listen and notice the word stress (•) in the countries and nationalities in **3a**.

Brazil   Brazilian

b PRONUNCIATION Listen again and practise. Copy the word stress.

Reading and Listening

5 **a** CD1 15 Read and listen to conversations 3, 4 and 5. Write the countries.

b Work in pairs. Compare answers.

1
LISA Hello, Tom.
TOM Hi, Lisa. How are you?
LISA I'm fine, thanks. And you?
TOM I'm OK, thanks.

2
PAOLO Bianca, this is Toshi.
BIANCA Hello, Toshi. Nice to meet you.
TOSHI You too.

3
RECEPTIONIST Good morning. What's your name, please?
CARLOS It's Carlos Moreno.
RECEPTIONIST And where are you from?
CARLOS I'm from _____ .

HELP WITH GRAMMAR
be (1): positive and *Wh-* questions

6 **a** Fill in the gaps with *'m, 're* or *'s.*

POSITIVE (+)

1	I _'m_ from Spain.	(= I am)
2	You_____ in room 6.	(= you are)
3	He_____ from Italy.	(= he is)
4	She_____ from Brazil.	(= she is)
5	It_____ Carlos Moreno.	(= it is)
6	We_____ from Australia.	(= we are)
7	They_____ from the UK.	(= they are)

b Fill in the gaps with *are* or *'s.*

WH- QUESTIONS (?)

1 Where _are_ you from?   4 What_____ your name?
2 Where_____ he from?   5 What _____ your names?
3 Where_____ she from?   6 Where _____ they from?

c Check in **GRAMMAR 1.1** ▶ p129.

> **4**
> RECEPTIONIST What are your names, please?
> DANIEL My name's Daniel Ross and this is Kelly Easton.
> RECEPTIONIST Where are you from?
> DANIEL We're from _____ .
> RECEPTIONIST Welcome to the conference. You're in room 6.

> **5**
> EMMA Where's he from?
> DAVE He's from _____ .
> EMMA OK. And where's she from?
> DAVE She's from _____ .
> EMMA Right. And where are they from?
> DAVE They're from _____ , I think.

7 **a** **CD1** ▶16 **PRONUNCIATION** Listen and practise the sentences in **6a** and the questions in **6b**. Copy the contractions (*I'm, you're, What's,* etc.).

I'm from Spain.

b Work in pairs. Practise conversations 3, 4 and 5.

8 Fill in the gaps with *'m, 're, are* or *'s.*

> EMMA Where [1] _are_ they from?
> DAVE They[2]_____ from Egypt.
> EMMA What [3]_____ **their** names?
> DAVE **His** name[4]_____ Hanif and **her** name[5]_____ Fatima.
>
> RECEPTIONIST What [6]_____ **your** names, please?
> DIETER **Our** names [7]_____ Dieter Koller and Mehmet Kaya.
> RECEPTIONIST Where [8]_____ you from?
> DIETER I[9]_____ from Germany and he[10]_____ from Turkey.

HELP WITH GRAMMAR
Subject pronouns and possessive adjectives

9 Fill in the table with the words in **bold** in **8**.

subject pronouns	I	you	he	she	it	we	they
possessive adjectives	my				its		

GRAMMAR 1.2 ▶ p129

10 **a** Choose the correct words.

> RECEPTIONIST What are [1]*you/your* names, please?
> MARTIN [2]*We/Our* names are Martin and Julia Green.
> RECEPTIONIST Where are [3]*you/your* from?
> MARTIN [4]*We/Our* 're from the USA.
>
> LISA Where are [5]*they/their* from?
> TOM [6]*He/His* 's from France and [7]*she/her* 's from Japan.
> LISA What are [8]*they/their* names?
> TOM [9]*He/His* name's Louis and [10]*she/her* name's Hiroko.

b Work in pairs. Compare answers.

Get ready ... Get it right!

11 Work in pairs. Student A p104. Student B p109.

Vocabulary jobs; *a* and *an*
Grammar *be* (2): negative, *yes/no* questions and short answers

QUICK REVIEW Numbers 0–20
Work in pairs. Count from 0 to 20:
A *Zero.* B *One.* A *Two.* B *Three.*
Then count backwards from 20 to 0:
A *Twenty.* B *Nineteen.* A *Eighteen.*

Listening and Speaking

1 a Work in pairs. Look at A–D. How do we say the phone numbers?

TIP • In phone numbers 0 = *oh* or *zero* and 11 = *double one.*

b CD1 17 **PRONUNCIATION** Listen and check. Listen again and practise.

2 a CD1 18 Listen to four conversations. Write the phone numbers.

b Ask three students their phone numbers. You can invent numbers if you like!

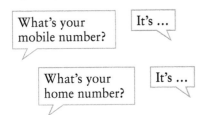

What's your mobile number? | It's …

What's your home number? | It's …

Vocabulary and Speaking
Jobs

3 a Work in pairs. Which of these jobs do you know? Then do the exercise in VOCABULARY 1.2 p128.

a manager   a doctor   an engineer
a sales assistant   a waiter/a waitress
a cleaner   a police officer
an actor/an actress   a musician
a teacher   a student   a housewife
an accountant   a lawyer
a builder   a mechanic

TIPS • In these vocabulary boxes we only show the main stress.
• We can also say *I'm unemployed.* not ~~I'm an unemployed.~~ and *I'm retired.* not ~~I'm a retired.~~

b CD1 19 **PRONUNCIATION** Listen and practise. Copy the word stress.

HELP WITH VOCABULARY *a* and *an*

4 Look at the jobs in **3a**. Then complete the rules with *a* or *an*.

● We use _____ with nouns that begin with a **consonant** sound. (The consonants are *b, c, d, f,* etc.)

● We use _____ with nouns that begin with a **vowel** sound. (The vowels are *a, e, i, o, u.*)

VOCABULARY 1.3 ▶ p128

5 Fill in the gaps with *a* or *an*.

1 _____ job   4 _____ book
2 _____ student   5 _____ English book
3 _____ answer   6 _____ room

6 a Look again at the pictures in VOCABULARY 1.2 ▶ p128. Take turns to cover the words and test your partner.

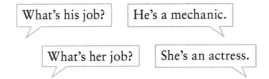

What's his job? | He's a mechanic.

What's her job? | She's an actress.

b What's your job? Ask other students.

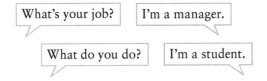

What's your job? | I'm a manager.

What do you do? | I'm a student.

Listening and Speaking

7 **a** `CD1` **20** Read and listen to these conversations. Fill in the gaps with the correct jobs.

1 A Are you from New York?
   B No, we aren't from the USA. We're from Canada.
   A Oh, really? What do you do?
   B I'm an ¹_____ and Jane's a ²_____ .

2 A Who's she?
   B Her name's Sally Andrews.
   A Is she a ³_____ ?
   B Yes, she is. But she isn't famous.

3 A What do you do?
   B I'm a ⁴_____ . And you?
   A I'm an ⁵_____ .
   B Are you from Mexico?
   A No, I'm not. I'm from Colombia.

b Look at the photo. Match conversations 1–3 to the groups of people A–C.

> **HELP WITH GRAMMAR**
> *be* (2): negative, *yes/no* questions and short answers

8 **a** Look again at **7a**. <u>Underline</u> all the parts of *be* in the conversations.

b Fill in the gaps in these negative sentences with *'m, aren't* and *isn't*.

1 I _____ not a teacher.
2 You/We/They _____ from the USA. (= are not)
3 He/She/It _____ famous. (= is not)

c Fill in the gaps in these questions and answers with *'m, Is, Are, isn't* or *aren't*.

1 _Are_ you from Spain?
   Yes, I am./No, I _____ not.
2 _____ she a musician?
   Yes, she is./No, she _____ .
3 _____ you from New York?
   Yes, we are./No, we _____ .

d Check in `GRAMMAR 1.3` p129.

9 `CD1` **21** `PRONUNCIATION` Listen and practise. Copy the contractions (*I'm, aren't,* etc.).

I'm not a teacher.

We aren't from the USA.

10 Work in pairs. Ask and answer questions about the people in the photo.

> Is he a doctor?

> No, he isn't. He's an engineer.

11 **a** Tick (✓) the sentences that are true for you. Make the other sentences negative. Write the correct sentences.

1 I'm an English student. ✓
2 I'm from the UK.
   I'm not from the UK. I'm from Poland.
3 My English class is in room 12.
4 I'm an accountant.
5 My teacher's from Australia.
6 My language school is in London.
7 My English lessons are on Tuesdays and Thursdays.
8 The students in my class are all from my country.

b Work in groups. Compare sentences.

Get ready ... Get it right!

12 Work in pairs. Student A p104. Student B p109.

QUICK REVIEW **Jobs** Work in pairs. Write all the jobs you know. Which pair in the class has the most words?

What number is it?

1 a Work in pairs. How do we say these numbers? Check in VOCABULARY 1.4 ▶ p128.

| 20 | 30 | 40 | 50 | 60 | 70 | 80 | 90 | 100 |

b Work in the same pairs. Say these numbers.

| 28 | 34 | 47 | 51 | 63 | 75 | 86 | 92 |

2 a CD1 ▶ 22 Listen to these numbers. Notice the stress.

| thirteen | thirty | fifteen | fifty | nineteen | ninety |

b CD1 ▶ 23 Listen and write the numbers.

c CD1 ▶ 24 **PRONUNCIATION** Listen and practise the numbers in **2a** and **2b**.

3 Work in pairs. Say a number between 1 and 100. Your partner says the next three numbers.

fifty-eight

fifty-nine, sixty, sixty-one

What's her address?

4 a Look at the photo of Emma. Then match these words to Emma's things 1–3.

a credit card   a business card   a mobile phone

b Match these words/phrases to the letters a–j in the pictures.

1 first name *b*
2 surname
3 home number
4 work number
5 mobile number
6 home address
7 email address
8 postcode at work
9 credit card number
10 job

c Work in pairs. Ask questions about 1–10 in **4b**.

What's her first name?   Emma.

1 Webber & Webber Ltd

89 Villiers Street
Liverpool
a L14 6Y2

b Emma Mitchell
c Sales Manager

d Tel **0151 496 0814**
e Mobile **07974 610771**
f email **emma.mitchell@wwl.co.uk**

2
HOME BANK
CREDIT

g 4589 2300 6754 7961
4550

VALID FROM 02/12   EXPIRES END 01/20

MRS EMMA R MITCHELL **h**

3

Hi Daniela!
The party's at my house. My address is
i 68 Evesham Road Liverpool L13 7KW.
My home number is
j 0151 496 0633.
See you on Sunday!
Love Emma

Hiring a car

Sentence stress (1)

5 CD1 ▶25 Look at the photo of Paul. Then listen to the woman's questions. Notice the sentence stress. We stress the important words.

1 What's your surname, please?
2 What's your first name?
3 And what's your nationality?
4 What's your address?
5 And what's your postcode?
6 What's your mobile number?
7 And what's your home number?
8 What's your email address?

6 a VIDEO ▶1 CD1 ▶26 Watch or listen to Paul's conversation. Tick (✓) the sentences in **5** when you hear them.

b Watch or listen again. Complete the form.

Car Hire Form
SBP Car Rentals

Customer ref: 00349

surname	
first name	*Paul*
nationality	
address	*Road*
	Bristol
mobile number	*07969*
home number	
email address	*paul99@webmail.com*

REAL WORLD Asking people to repeat things

7 a CD1 ▶27 Listen to these sentences from the conversation in the car hire office. Fill in the gaps with these words.

> repeat   again   please   Could   sorry

1 I'm _____ ?
2 _____ you say that _____ , please?
3 Could you _____ that, _____ ?

b PRONUNCIATION Listen again and practise.

REAL WORLD 1.3 ▶ p129

8 CD1 ▶28 PRONUNCIATION Listen and practise the questions in **5**. Copy the sentence stress.

9 Work in pairs. Interview your partner and fill in the form. Use the questions in **5**.

Car Hire Form
SBP Car Rentals

Customer ref: 00350

surname	
first name	
nationality	
address	
mobile number	
home number	
email address	

1 Look at the picture of the lost
property room in the conference
hotel. Match these words to 1–17.

diaries *12*   wallets
an MP3 player   a mobile
watches   an umbrella   bags
shoes   a camera   coats
a bike/bicycle   a radio
suitcases   a laptop
dresses   ID cards   false teeth

HELP WITH VOCABULARY
Plurals

2 **a** Write the missing letters. When
do we add *-s*, *-es* and *-ies*? Which
plurals are irregular?

singular	plural
a bag	bag _
a wallet	wallet _
a suitcase	suitcase _
a watch	watch _ _
a dress	dress _ _
a diary	diar _ _ _ _
a man	m _ n
a woman	wom _ n
a child	childr _ n
a person	p _ _ _ ple
a tooth	t _ _ _ th

b Check in VOCABULARY 1.6 ▶ p128.

3 CD1 ▶ 29 PRONUNCIATION Listen
and practise the singular and plural
words in **2a**.

4 Write the plurals.

a a bike *bikes*   **f** a camera
b a credit card   **g** an address
c a nationality   **h** a man
d a waitress   **i** a country
e a person   **j** a woman

5 Work in pairs. Take turns to test each other on 1–17.

Number 12.   They're diaries.

Number 17.   It's an MP3 player.

6 Eva's got a job at the hotel. Look at the pictures and fill in the gaps with words from **1**.

A

What's this in English?

It's an _____ .

B

What's that in English?

It's a _____ .

C

What are these in English?

They're _____ .

D

What are those?!

They're _____ !

HELP WITH VOCABULARY
this, that, these, those

7 Fill in the table with *this, that, these* and *those*.

	here ↓	there ↗
singular		
plural		

8 a CD1 30 PRONUNCIATION Listen and practise. Copy the stress.

this → *What's this?* → *What's this in English?*

b Choose three things in the classroom or from your bag. Ask your teacher what they are in English.

What's that in English?   It's a poster.

What are these in English?   They're keys.

HELP WITH PRONUNCIATION
Word stress and syllables

1 CD1 31 Listen to these words. Notice the stress and number of syllables. Listen again and practise.

Brit-ish   Ja-pàn

bi-cy-cle   com-pù-ter   sev-en-teèn

2 a Work in pairs. Write the words in the table.

teacher	musician	address	thirty
thirteen	umbrella	engineer	manager
Brazil	Germany	Japanese	mobile
Mexican	mechanic	unemployed	

Brit-ish	*teacher*
Ja-pàn	
bi-cy-cle	
com-pù-ter	
sev-en-teèn	

b CD1 32 Listen and check. Listen again and practise.

3 a Write five words. Mark the stress on each word.

b Work in pairs. Compare words. Is the stress on your partner's words correct?

continue2learn

▶ **Vocabulary, Grammar and Real World**
- **Extra Practice 1 and Progress Portfolio 1** p115
- **Language Summary 1** p128
- **1A–D** Workbook p5
- **Self-study DVD-ROM 1** with Review Video

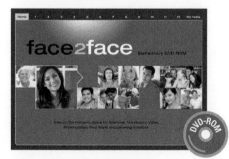

▶ **Reading and Writing**
- **Portfolio 1** At the hotel Workbook p64
  Reading addresses; hotel registration forms
  Writing capital letters (1); addresses; filling in a hotel registration form

2A ▶ What's important?

Vocabulary adjectives (1); adjective
word order and *very*
Grammar *have got*: positive and
negative, questions and short answers

QUICK REVIEW Personal possessions
What's in the lost property room at the conference hotel? Write all the things you can remember. Work in pairs. Compare lists. Then check on p14.

Vocabulary Adjectives (1)

1 **a** Tick the adjectives you know. Then do the exercise in **VOCABULARY 2.1** ▶ p130.

new	old	big	small
good	bad	early	late
cheap	expensive	fast	slow
beautiful	ugly	young	old
easy	difficult	right	wrong

nice	great	important	favourite

b Work in pairs. Take turns to test your partner on the opposites.

old   new

HELP WITH VOCABULARY
Adjective word order and *very*

2 Look at these sentences. Then choose the correct words in the rules.

She's late.

It's a small bag.

It's a very difficult question.

Those are my new shoes.

● We put adjectives *before/after* the verb *be*.
● We put adjectives *before/after* a noun.
● We put *very before/after* adjectives.
● Adjectives *are/aren't* plural with plural nouns.

VOCABULARY 2.2 ▶ p130

3 **a** Make sentences with these words.

1 very / 's / It / early .
   It's very early.
2 answer / right / That / 's / the .
3 very / are / Those / dresses / expensive .
4 cheap / a / It / watch / 's .
5 very / They / good / 're / cameras .
6 question / very / a / difficult / 's / That .

b Work in pairs. Compare sentences.

ALAN What things are important in my life? Well, I've got <u>an old car</u>. It isn't very fast, but I love it. What else? Well, my mobile's very important to me. It's got all my friends' phone numbers on it, my photos, music, everything! I haven't got a laptop, but I've got an old computer. That's important to me for school. And I've got a big TV in my room. That's very important because I love football!

Reading and Listening

4 **a** **CD1 33** Read and listen to Alan and his grandmother, Mary. <u>Underline</u> the things that are important to each person.

b Read the texts again. Find all the adjectives.

c Work in pairs. Compare answers.

HELP WITH GRAMMAR *have got:* positive and negative

5 **a** Look again at the texts about Alan and Mary. Find all the examples of *'ve got* (= *have got*), *'s got* (= *has got*), *haven't got* and *hasn't got*.

b Fill in the gaps with *'ve*, *'s*, *haven't* and *hasn't*.

POSITIVE (+)

I / you / we / they _____ got (= have got)
he / she / it _____ got (= has got)

NEGATIVE (–)

I / you / we / they _____ got (= have not got)
he / she / it _____ got (= has not got)

GRAMMAR 2.1 ▶ p131

MARY What's important to me? I've got this very expensive watch. It's from Ben, my husband, and I love it. And my diary – that's important to me too. Ben hasn't got a diary, he's got everything on his mobile these days. And my new bicycle is important to me because we haven't got a car. What else? Well, we've got a beautiful cat, Lily. She's very important!

6 CD1 ▶ 34 PRONUNCIATION Listen and practise. Copy the stress and contractions (*I've*, *he's*, etc.).
I've got an old car.

7 Fill in the gaps with the correct form of *have got*.

1 I _'ve got_ (+) a new camera.
2 She_____ (–) a very big house.
3 You_____ (+) a nice car.
4 We _____ (–) a computer.
5 I _____ (–) your mobile number.
6 He_____ (+) a very good TV, but he _____ (–) a DVD player.
7 Mary and Ben _____ (+) a beautiful cat called Lily.
8 They _____ (–) a dog.

8 **a** Think of a friend and write five things he/she has got or hasn't got.

b Work in pairs. Compare lists. Are any of the things the same?

Listening and Speaking

9 **a** Work in pairs. Look at the table and guess which things Alan and Mary have got. Put a tick (✓) or a cross (✗) in the *guess* columns.

	Alan		Mary	
product	guess	answer	guess	answer
laptop	✗	✗		
camera				
MP3 player				
radio				
DVD player				

b CD1 ▶ 35 Listen to Alan and Mary answer questions for a survey. Complete the *answer* columns. Are your guesses correct?

HELP WITH GRAMMAR
have got: questions and short answers

10 **a** Fill in the gaps with *have*, *has*, *haven't* or *hasn't*.

QUESTIONS	SHORT ANSWERS
Have you got a camera?	Yes, I _____ . No, I _____ .
_____ he/she got a DVD player?	Yes, he/she _____ . No, he/she _____ .
_____ they got any cheap TVs?	Yes, they _____ . No, they _____ .
What _____ you got in your bag?	

TIP • We use *any* with plural nouns in *yes/no* questions.

b Check in GRAMMAR 2.2 ▶ p131.

11 CD1 ▶ 36 PRONUNCIATION Listen and practise the questions and short answers in **10a**.

12 Work in pairs. Ask questions about Alan and Mary.

Has Alan got a new car?   No, he hasn't.

Get ready … Get it right!

13 Work in pairs. Student A p104. Student B p109.

QUICK REVIEW *have got* **Work in pairs. Ask questions with *have got*. Find five things you've got but your partner hasn't got.**

Ben   Mary

husband   ~~son~~   daughter   father
mother   brother   children

PAM We're a typical British family, I think. My
¹ *husband* 's name is Nick and we've got two
² _____ , a boy and a girl. Our ³ *son* 's name is
Robbie and Florence is our ⁴ _____ – she's just
a baby. And my parents? Well, Ben is my ⁵ _____
and Mary is my ⁶ _____ . I've got one
⁷ _____ , his name's Greg, and one sister, Jill.

~~wife~~   ~~parents~~   sisters   granddaughter
grandsons   grandchildren

GREG My ⁸ *wife* 's name is Martina and we've got
one son, Alan. He's nineteen years old now. I've got
two ⁹ _____ , Pam and Jill. Pam's married
with two kids and Jill's divorced. My ¹⁰ *parents* '
names are Ben and Mary. They've got three children
and three ¹¹ _____ , two ¹² _____ ,
Alan and Robbie, and a ¹³ _____ , Florence.

Nick   Pam

Jill

Greg   Martina

Robbie   Florence

aunts   ~~grandparents~~   cousins
grandmother   grandfather   uncle

ALAN My mum and dad's names are Greg and
Martina. I've got two ¹⁴ *aunts* , Pam and Jill, and
one ¹⁵ _____ . His name's Nick and he's a
doctor. I've also got two ¹⁶ _____ , Robbie and
Florence. My ¹⁷ *grandparents* ' names are Ben – he's
my ¹⁸ _____ – and Mary, my ¹⁹ _____ .

Alan

Vocabulary, Reading and Listening
Family

1 **a** Look at the family tree. Then read about the family. Fill in the gaps with the words in the boxes.

   b **CD1 ▶37** Listen and check your answers.

2 Look again at the family tree. Put the words in the boxes in three groups. Then check in **VOCABULARY 2.3 ▶ p130**.

   1 ♂ male *father/dad*

   2 ♀ female *mother/mum*

   3 ♂♀ male and female *parents*

3 **a** Write four questions with *How many ... ?* about the people in the family tree.

   How many brothers and sisters has Pam got?

   How many children have Mary and Ben got?

   b Work in pairs. Ask and answer your questions.

4 Tick the correct sentences. Change the words in bold in the incorrect sentences.

   1 Jill is Pam's ~~cousin~~. *sister*

   2 Ben is Mary's **husband**.

   3 Jill is Alan's **cousin**.

   4 Alan is Martina's **son**.

   5 Nick and Pam are Robbie's **grandparents**.

   6 Mary is Robbie and Florence's **grandmother**.

5 **a** Look at these sentences. Then read the rule.

Jill is Pam's sister.   My husband's name is Nick.

● We use a name + **'s** (*Pam's*, etc.) or a noun + **'s** (*husband's*, etc.) for the possessive.

b *'s* can mean *is*, *has* or the possessive. Match 1–3 to a–c.

1 Ben is Pam**'s** father.   **a**   *'s = is*
2 Jill**'s** her sister.   **b**   *'s = has*
3 She**'s** got one brother.   **c**   *'s = possessive*

GRAMMAR 2.3 ▶ p131

6 Make sentences about these people.

1 Pam / Alan   3 Robbie / Florence
   Pam is Alan's aunt.   4 Mary / Ben
2 Greg / Martina   5 Florence / Ben and Mary

7 CD1 ▶38 PRONUNCIATION Listen and practise. Copy the stress.

Ȧlan's → Pȧm is Ȧlan's ȧunt.

Listening and Speaking

8 Jill wants to show her new boyfriend, Luke, some photos. Look at photos A–D. Who are the people?

A

B

C

D

9 **a** CD1 ▶39 Listen to Jill and Luke's conversation. Put photos A–D in order.

b Listen again and choose the correct words.

1 Jill's sister Pam is an (*English*)/*French* teacher.
2 Pam's husband Nick is a *lawyer/doctor*.
3 Their son Robbie is *six/seven*.
4 Jill's brother Greg is an *engineer/accountant*.
5 His wife Martina is *Spanish/Italian*.
6 Jill's mother is *retired/a sales assistant*.
7 Jill's father is *seventy/seventy-three*.

10 **a** CD1 ▶39 Listen to the first sentence of the conversation again. Notice the sentence stress. We stress the important words.

Lu̇ke, co̊me and lo̊ok at the̊se pho̊tos of my fåmily.

b Look at Audio Script CD1 ▶39 p157. Listen to the whole conversation and follow the stressed words.

Get ready … Get it right!

11 **a** Write your name and the names of five people in your family on a piece of paper. Think what you can say about these people (age, job, married, etc.). Don't write this information.

b Choose a partner, but don't talk to him/her. Swap papers. Make questions to ask about your partner's family.

Who's (Claudia)?

Is she married?

Has she got any children?

12 **a** Work with your partner. Take turns to ask questions about his/her family. Make notes on your partner's answers.

b Tell another student about your partner's family.

▷ REAL
2C WORLD ▷ **Time and money**

Real World telling the time; talking about the time; saying prices; buying tickets at the cinema
Vocabulary time words

What's the time?

1 **a** Put these time words in order.

> a minute   a year   a day   a week
> an hour   a second   *1*   a month

b Work in pairs. Ask and answer these questions.

1 How many minutes are in an hour?
2 How many hours are in a day?
3 How many months are in a year?
4 How many weeks are in a year?
5 How many hours are in a week?
6 How many days are in a year?

2 **a** Match the times to pictures A–F.

> one o'clock *A*   quarter to ten   twenty past five
> half past seven   quarter past four   twenty to nine

b We can say times in a different way. Match these times to pictures A–F.

> four fifteen   five twenty   seven thirty
> eight forty   nine forty-five   one

3 **a** Complete the times.

1 five past _____   2 twenty-five to _____   3 ten _____

4 _____ _____ eleven   5 _____ -five   6 _____ _____

b Check in **REAL WORLD 2.1** ▷ p131.

4 **CD1 ▷ 40** Listen and match conversations 1–3 to three of the pictures A–F in **2a**.

REAL WORLD Talking about the time

5 **a** Fill in the gaps in the questions and answers.

> What time ¹_____ it?
>
> It's ²_____ o'clock.
>
> What's the ³_____, please?
>
> It's about half ⁴_____ seven.
>
> Excuse me. Have you ⁵_____ the time, please?
>
> Yes, it's four fifteen.

b Fill in the gaps with *to, from* or *at*.

1 My English class is _____ ten.
2 My son's class is _____ seven _____ nine thirty.

REAL WORLD 2.2 ▷ p132

6 **a** **CD1 ▷ 41** **PRONUNCIATION** Listen and practise the questions and answers in **5a**. Copy the polite intonation in the questions.

b Write six times. Work in pairs. Ask and answer the questions in **5a**. Write your partner's times. Are they correct?

BRENT GALLERY
Mexican Art

July 20th–September 3rd

Opening times
10.00–¹ _____ Mon-Fri
10.00–² _____ Sat & Sun

Adults ª£9.50/£10.50

Children ᵇ£5.60/£6.50

Ticket office: 08081 570570

Book online: www.brentgallery.org.uk **A**

FilmWorld

Acton Lane, London W3 5HU

Now showing

A New Day (12)
³ _____ , 7.00, 9.20

The Brothers (15)
5.00, ⁴ _____ , 9.30

Tickets: Adults ᶜ£10.50/£11.50
Children ᵈ£7.25/£8.25

For more information phone
08081 570203
www.filmworld.co.uk **B**

An evening out

7 **a** Look at adverts A and B. Which is for a cinema and which is for an exhibition?

b [CD1 42] Listen and write the missing times 1–4 on the adverts.

8 **a** Work in pairs. How do we say these prices?

| £20 | £7.50 | 40p | £29.99 |
| €9 | €6.50 | $35 | 50c |

b [CD1 43] [PRONUNCIATION] Listen and check. Listen again and practise.

c [CD1 44] Listen and choose the correct ticket prices a–d on adverts A and B.

9 **a** Before you watch or listen, check these words with your teacher.

| buy popcorn a screen start |

b [VIDEO 2] [CD1 45] Look at the photo in a cinema. Watch or listen to the people's conversations with the ticket seller. Which film do Chris and Louise want to see? Which film do Alison and Josh want to see?

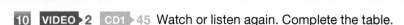

Alison *Josh* *Louise* *Chris*

10 [VIDEO 2] [CD1 45] Watch or listen again. Complete the table.

	price of tickets	time film starts	screen number
Chris and Louise			
Alison and Josh			

REAL WORLD Buying tickets at the cinema

11 **a** Read the sentences. Fill in the gaps with these words.

| ~~Can~~ adults time are |
| Thanks please is welcome |

CUSTOMER		TICKET SELLER

CUSTOMER

¹ _Can_ I have (two) tickets for (*The Brothers*), please?
(Two) tickets for (*A New Day*), ² _____ . One adult and one child.

How much ³ _____ that?
How much ⁴ _____ the tickets?

Here you are. What ⁶ _____ is the film?

Right. ⁷ _____ a lot.
Thank you very much.

TICKET SELLER

Yes, of course.

That's (£23), please.
(£11.50) for ⁵ _____ and (£8.45) for children. So that's (£19.95), please.

It starts at (seven fifteen).
It starts in (two minutes).

You're ⁸ _____ . Enjoy the film.

b Check in [REAL WORLD 2.4] p132.

12 [CD1 46] Listen and practise the customer's sentences in **11a**.

13 Work in pairs. Student A p105. Student B p110.

QUICK REVIEW Times and prices Write four times and four prices. Work in pairs. Say them to your partner. He/She writes them down. Are they correct?

1 Work in pairs. Which of these words do you know? Then do the exercise in **VOCABULARY 2.5** p130.

> a mirror   a desk   a sofa   a carpet   a door   a bookcase
> a window   the floor   a plant   a coffee table   a lamp   curtains

HELP WITH VOCABULARY Prepositions of place

2 Where's the cat? Match the prepositions to pictures 1–6. Then check in **VOCABULARY 2.6** p131.

> in   on   by   under   behind   in front of

 1
 2
 3
 4
 5
 6

3 a Look at the picture. Choose six of these things. Write sentences to say where they are.

Nick's suitcase is behind the sofa.

> Nick's suitcase
> Nick's keys
> Nick's mobile phone
> Pam's coat
> Robbie's new shoes
> the cat
> Robbie's bag
> Robbie's books
> Nick's passport
> Robbie's MP3 player
> the lamp
> the DVDs

b Work in pairs. Compare sentences. Are your partner's sentences correct?

4 Work in pairs. Cover the box in **3a**. Point at things in the picture and ask questions with *Whose ...?*

> Whose mobile phone is this?

> It's Nick's.

> Whose shoes are these?

> They're Robbie's.

5 a CD1 47 Listen and tick the things in the box in **3a** that the family talk about.

b Listen again. Three things are in the wrong place in the picture. What are they?

c Where's the baby?!

6 Look at Audio Script CD1 47 p157. Listen again and underline all the prepositions of place.

7 Look at the picture for one minute. Then cover the picture. Work in pairs. Take turns to ask where things are in the living room.

> Where's Robbie's bag?

> It's by the door.

1 a CD1 48 The schwa /ə/ is very common in English. Listen to these words. Notice the schwas. Is the schwa stressed?

address	mechanic	Poland	teacher
/ə/	/ə/	/ə/	/ə/

doctor	number	manager	accountant
/ə/	/ə/	/ə//ə/	/ə/

b Listen again and practise.

2 a Work in pairs. Underline the schwa in each word.

> China   seven   actor   important   second
> daughter   parents   Japan   police   sofa

b CD1 49 Listen and check. Listen again and practise.

3 a Look at these words. Circle the word with a schwa.

1 email / letter   5 laptop / computer
2 dentist / cleaner   6 Italy / Egypt
3 seventy / ninety   7 window / mirror
4 Spanish / German   8 Saturday / Tuesday

b Work in pairs. Compare answers.

c CD1 50 Listen and check. Listen again and practise.

continue2learn

▶ **Vocabulary, Grammar and Real World**

■ **Extra Practice 2 and Progress Portfolio 2** p116
■ **Language Summary 2** p130
■ **2A–D** Workbook 2 p10
■ **Self-study DVD-ROM 2** with Review Video

▶ **Reading and Writing**

■ **Portfolio 2** My favourite thing Workbook p66
Reading people's favourite things
Writing capital letters (2); punctuation; a description of your favourite thing

3A ▶ My day

Vocabulary daily routines
Grammar Present Simple (1): positive and
Wh- questions (*I/you/we/they*)

Vocabulary Daily routines

1 **a** Tick the words/phrases you know. Then do
the exercise in **VOCABULARY 3.1** ▶ p132.

> get up   go to bed   leave home   get home
> have breakfast   have lunch   have dinner
> start work/classes   finish work/classes
> work   study   sleep   live

TIP • In these vocabulary boxes we only show the
main stress in phrases.

b Match two of the words/phrases from **1a** to
these times of day.

1 in the morning *get up*   **3** in the evening

2 in the afternoon   **4** at night

c Work in pairs. Compare answers. Are they
the same?

Reading and Speaking

2 **a** Look at the photos of Kari Matchett. What's
her job?

b Before you read, check these words/phrases
with your teacher.

> glamorous   a TV show   a studio
> hair   make-up   learn your lines

c Work in pairs. Guess the times that TV actors
do these things.

1 get up   **3** start work
2 have breakfast   **4** have lunch

d Read the article and check your answers.

3 Read the article again. Are these sentences true
(T) or false (F)? Correct the false sentences.

       Canada
1 Kari Matchett is from ~~Los Angeles~~. *F*
2 TV actors get up very late.
3 They have breakfast at the studio.
4 They work for six hours before lunch.
5 They have half an hour for lunch.

**This week I talk to Kari Matchett, star of the TV
shows *24* and *ER*, about a typical day at the studio
and her glamorous life as an actress.**

DAVID Where are you
from, Kari?
KARI I'm from Canada, but
I live and work in Los
Angeles.
D Can you tell us about your
day-to-day life?
K Well, TV actors work very
long days and we start work
very early.
D What time do you get up?
K I get up at 4.30 in the
morning.
D Wow! You get up very early.

HELP WITH GRAMMAR
Present Simple (1): positive (*I/you/we/they*)

● We use the Present Simple to talk about daily routines.

4 **a** Find the verbs in these sentences. They are in
the Present Simple.

1 I get up at 4.30 in the morning.
2 You get up very early.
3 We start work at about 7.00.
4 They have an hour for lunch.

b Is the Present Simple the same or different after
I, you, we and *they*?

GRAMMAR 3.1 ▶ p134

5 **CD1** ▶ **51** **PRONUNCIATION** Listen and practise the sentences
in **4a**. Copy the stress.

I get up at four thirty in the morning.

6 **a** Look at Kari's answers in the article again. Underline all
the verbs in the Present Simple.

b Work in pairs. Compare answers.

K Yes, and I'm not very good in the morning, so it's always difficult! I leave home at 5.30 and I get to the studio at about 6.00. That's when people do my hair and make-up.

D What about breakfast?

K I have breakfast at about 6.15 in the make-up room. Then we start work at about 7.00.

D When do you have lunch?

K We have lunch at 1.00 and we start work again at 2.00.

7 Read about Kari's afternoon and evening routine. Fill in the gaps with these verbs.

| ~~finish~~   get   go   start   finish   sleep |

D When do you finish work?

K Most days we ¹ *finish* at about 9.00.

D You ² _____ work at 7.00 and you ³ _____ work at 9.00!

K Yes, it's a very long day, but sometimes I ⁴ _____ for an hour in the afternoon.

D What time do you get home?

K I ⁵ _____ home at about 9.30.

D Where do you have dinner?

K Usually at home while I learn my lines for the next day. Then I ⁶ _____ to bed at 11.00.

D So do you have a glamorous life?

K Not when I'm at work, no – definitely not!

8 a Write six sentences about your daily routine. Use words/phrases from **1a**.

I start work at half past eight.

b Work in pairs. Compare sentences.

HELP WITH GRAMMAR Present Simple (1): *Wh-* questions (*I/you/we/they*)

9 a Look at the table. Notice the word order in questions.

question word	auxiliary	subject	infinitive	
What time	do	you	get up?	
When	do	you	have	lunch?

TIP • Present Simple questions are the same for *I, you, we* and *they*.

b Write questions 1–3 in the table.

1 When do you finish work?
2 What time do you get home?
3 Where do you have dinner?

c Check in **GRAMMAR 3.2** p134.

10 a Make questions with these words.

1 Where / live / you / do ? *Where do you live?*
2 you / do / Where / work ?
3 What time / get up / you / do ?
4 start / When / do / you / work or classes ?
5 do / What time / get / you / home ?
6 dinner / do / When / you / have ?

b **CD1 ▸ 52** **PRONUNCIATION** Listen and check. Notice how we say *do you* /djə/. Then listen again and practise.

Where do you /djə/ live?

c Work in pairs. Ask and answer the questions in **10a**.

Get ready ... Get it right!

11 Write eight questions about people's routines in the week or at the weekend. Use words/phrases from **1a**.

What time do you go to bed in the week?

When do you get up at the weekend?

12 a Ask other students your questions. For each question, find one student who does this at the same time as you.

b Tell the class two things that you and other students do at the same time.

QUICK REVIEW Daily routines Work in pairs. Ask and answer questions about your Sunday routines: A *What time do you get up on Sundays?* B *At about eleven. And you?* Are the times the same or different?

Vocabulary Free time activities (1)

1 a Work in pairs. Which of these phrases do you know? Then do the exercise in **VOCABULARY 3.2** p133.

> stay in   go out (a lot)   eat out
> go for a drink   go to the cinema
> go to concerts   go shopping
> phone friends/my family
> visit friends/my family
> have coffee with friends
> do (a lot of) sport
> watch (a lot of) TV/DVDs

b Work in new pairs. What are your five favourite things to do on Saturdays?

Listening

2 Look at the photo of Freddie and Jeanette. Where are they? Are they good friends, do you think?

3 a **CD1 53** Listen to Freddie and Jeanette's conversation. Are these sentences true (T) or false (F)?

1 Freddie and Jeanette are good friends. *F*
2 They work in the same office.
3 They watch a lot of DVDs.
4 Freddie's got tickets for a concert on Saturday.
5 Freddie and Jeanette are single.

b Listen again. Tick the things in **1a** that Jeanette does in her free time.

1 go out after work
2 watch TV in the evenings
3 go to the cinema
4 watch a lot of DVDs ✓
5 go shopping on Saturday morning
6 go out on Saturday evening
7 visit her parents on Sunday afternoon
8 go to concerts

HELP WITH GRAMMAR
Present Simple (2): negative (*I/you/we/they*)

4 a Look at the table. Notice the word order.

subject	auxiliary	infinitive	
I	don't (= do not)	go out	on Saturday evening.
You	don't	work	in this office.

b Write sentences 1 and 2 in the table.

1 We don't stay in at the weekend.
2 They don't watch TV in the day.

c Check in **GRAMMAR 3.3** p134.

5 a Tick the sentences that are true for you. Make the other sentences negative.

1 I study English. ✓
2 I phone my family every day
   I don't phone my family every day.
3 I go shopping on Saturdays.
4 I watch TV every evening.
5 I eat out with my friends a lot.
6 I live near this school.
7 I have lunch at 12.00 every day.
8 I work at the weekends.

b Work in pairs. Compare sentences.

HELP WITH GRAMMAR Present Simple (2): yes/no questions and short answers (I/you/we/they)

6 **a** Look at the table. Notice the word order in the questions.

YES/NO QUESTIONS (?)				SHORT ANSWERS
auxiliary	subject	infinitive		
Do	you	eat out	a lot?	Yes, I do. No, I don't.
				Yes, we _____ . No, we _____ .
				Yes, they _____ . No, they _____ .

b Write questions 1 and 2 in the table.

1 Do you go to concerts? 2 Do they watch TV a lot?

c Fill in the gaps in the *short answers* column with *do* or *don't*.

d Check in GRAMMAR 3.4 p134.

HELP WITH LISTENING
Weak forms (1): *do you … ?*

7 **a** CD1 54 Listen to how we usually say *do you*.

YOU EXPECT TO HEAR	YOU USUALLY HEAR
Do you /du: ju:/	Do you /djə/
Do you /du: ju:/ go out after work?	Do you /djə/ go out after work?

b CD1 55 Listen to these questions. Fill in the gaps. You will hear each sentence twice.

1 What _____ _____ _____ in the evenings?
2 _____ _____ _____ to the cinema?
3 What _____ _____ _____ at the weekends?
4 _____ _____ _____ to concerts?

8 **a** Fill in the gaps with *do, don't* or a verb from the box.

~~go out~~   visit   go out   watch   go (x2)

1 A *Do* you *go out* a lot in the week?
  B Yes, we _____ .
2 A _____ you _____ your parents at the weekend?
  B Yes, I _____ .
3 A _____ you _____ to concerts at the weekend?
  B No, we _____ .
4 A _____ you _____ shopping on Saturdays?
  B Yes, I _____ .
5 A _____ your parents _____ on Saturday evenings?
  B No, they _____ . They stay in and _____ TV.

b CD1 56 PRONUNCIATION Listen and check. Listen again and practise. Copy the stress and weak forms.

Do you /djə/ gȯ out a lȯt in the wėek?

c Work in pairs. Take turns to ask the questions in **8a**. Answer for you.

Vocabulary and Speaking
Time phrases with *on, in, at, every*

9 **a** Write these words and phrases in the correct place. Some words and phrases can go in more than one place. Then check in VOCABULARY 3.3 p133.

> ~~Saturday~~   ~~the morning~~   ~~nine o'clock~~
> ~~week~~   the afternoon   day
> the evening   month   half past three
> night   the week   Mondays
> Monday mornings   the weekend
> morning   Sunday afternoon

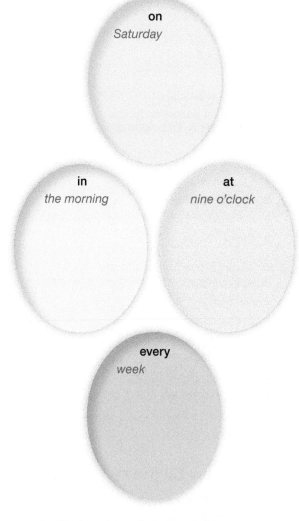

on
Saturday

in
the morning

at
nine o'clock

every
week

b Work in pairs. Test your partner.

| the weekend | | at the weekend |

Get ready … Get it right!

10 Work in two groups. Group A p105. Group B p110.

▶ REAL
3C WORLD ▶ Special days

Real World phrases for special days;
  talking about days and dates; suggestions
Vocabulary months; dates

Congratulations!

1 Match cards A–E to special days 1–5.

  1 a birthday
  2 a wedding
  3 the birth of a new baby
  4 a New Year's Eve party
  5 a wedding anniversary

2 a Match these phrases to the special days in **1**.

  Happy birthday!
  Happy New Year!
  Congratulations!
  Happy anniversary!

b CD1 57 **PRONUNCIATION** Listen and practise.

c CD1 58 Listen and answer with the correct phrase.

When's your birthday?

3 a Put the months in the correct order.

July	March	December
January *1*	April	October
August	June	February
November	May	September

b CD1 59 **PRONUNCIATION** Listen and check. Listen again and practise.

4 a Match the dates with the words. Then check in **VOCABULARY 3.5** p133.

1st	second	13th	twentieth
2nd	twelfth	20th	thirty-first
3rd	fourth	21st	thirtieth
4th	fifth	22nd	twenty-second
5th	first	30th	twenty-first
12th	third	31st	thirteenth

b CD1 60 **PRONUNCIATION** Listen and practise the dates in **4a**.

REAL WORLD Talking about days and dates

5 a Match questions 1–4 to answers a–d. Notice the words in bold.

  1 What day is it today?
  2 What's the date today?
  3 What's the date tomorrow?
  4 When's your birthday?

  a (It's) **the** fifth **of** March.
  b (It's) March **the** sixth.
  c (It's **on**) June the third.
  d It's Wednesday.

b CD1 61 **PRONUNCIATION** Listen and check. Listen again and practise.

REAL WORLD 3.2 p134

6 CD1 62 Listen to six conversations. Which dates do you hear?

  1 September 5th / 15th
  2 December 13th / 30th
  3 March 4th / 14th
  4 July 2nd / 22nd
  5 October 13th / 30th
  6 February 1st / 5th

7 a Write four dates that are important to you every year.

b Work in pairs. Say your dates to your partner. Write your partner's dates. Then ask why they are important.

> Why is May 6th important to you?

> Because it's my wedding anniversary.

Chris

Louise

What shall we get her?

8 **a** **VIDEO 3** **CD1 63** Watch or listen to Louise and her husband, Chris. What do they decide to buy their friend Sophie for her birthday?

b Watch or listen again and choose the correct answer.

1 The date today is the *19th/29th*.
2 It's Sophie's birthday on *Tuesday/Thursday*.
3 Louise *has got/hasn't got* Sophie a birthday card.
4 Sophie *has got/hasn't got* an MP3 player.
5 Sophie *has got/hasn't got* lots of books.
6 Sophie and Marcus *watch/don't watch* a lot of DVDs.

REAL WORLD Suggestions

9 Read these sentences. Fill in the gaps with these words.

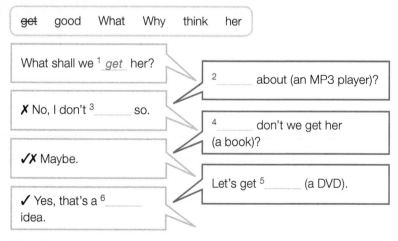

~~get~~	good	What	Why	think	her

What shall we ¹ *get* her?

² _____ about (an MP3 player)?

✗ No, I don't ³ _____ so.

⁴ _____ don't we get her (a book)?

✓✗ Maybe.

Let's get ⁵ _____ (a DVD).

✓ Yes, that's a ⁶ _____ idea.

TIP • We can say *get* or *buy*: *What shall we get/buy her?*

REAL WORLD 3.3 **p134**

10 **CD1 64** **PRONUNCIATION** Listen and practise the sentences in **9**.

What shall we get her?

11 Sophie and Marcus want to buy their son Liam a birthday present. Fill in the gaps with the correct words.

SOPHIE It's Liam's ¹ *birthday* next week. What ² _____ we get him?
MARCUS ³ _____ don't ⁴ _____ get him a laptop?
S No, I ⁵ _____ think ⁶ _____ . Let's ⁷ _____ him a new mobile.
M Maybe. But his mobile's only a year old.
S I know! What ⁸ _____ a new bike?
M Yes, ⁹ _____ a good ¹⁰ _____ .

12 **a** Work in pairs. It's Louise's birthday next week. Sophie and Marcus want to buy her a present. Write their conversation. Use language from **9**.

b Practise the conversation until you remember it.

c Work in groups of four. Role-play your conversations for the other pair. What present do the other pair choose?

VOCABULARY
3D AND SKILLS ▷ **Early bird?**

Vocabulary frequency adverbs
Grammar subject and object pronouns
Skills reading: a questionnaire;
listening: a conversation

QUICK REVIEW Dates Work in pairs. Take turns to say the dates 1st–31st: A *First.* B *Second.* A *Third* … . Then say them backwards! A *Thirty-first.* B *Thirtieth.* A *Twenty-ninth* … .

1 Put these frequency adverbs on the line. Then check in VOCABULARY 3.6 ▷ p133.

| hardly ever | never | always | sometimes | often | usually |

hardly ever

100%   0%

2 **a** Read the questionnaire. Tick your answers.

b Look at p114. What's your score? Are you an early bird or a night owl?

c Work in groups. Compare scores. How many of your answers are the same?

3 **a** CD1▷65 Listen to Jeanette and her husband, Dominic. Write *J* by Jeanette's answers to the questionnaire.

b Work in pairs. Compare answers. What's Jeanette's score? What kind of person is she?

HELP WITH VOCABULARY
Word order of frequency adverbs

4 **a** Underline the frequency adverbs (*often*, etc.) in the questionnaire.

b Choose the correct words in the rules.

• Frequency adverbs go *before/after* the verb *be*.

• Frequency adverbs go *before/after* other verbs.

VOCABULARY 3.7 ▷ p133.

5 **a** Put a frequency adverb in these sentences and make them true for you.

1 I get up at eight in the morning.
   I never get up at eight in the morning.
2 I have breakfast before 9 a.m.
3 I'm tired on Friday evenings.
4 I study English in the evening.
5 I'm happy on Monday mornings.
6 I go to the cinema at the weekend.
7 I'm late for my English class.
8 I watch TV on Sunday afternoons.

b Work in pairs. Compare sentences. How many are the same?

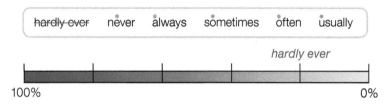

Are you an early bird or a night owl?
Do the questionnaire to find out!

1 When I get up in the morning ...
a I'm always happy and I have a lot of energy.
b I'm sometimes happy, but I don't have a lot of energy.
c I'm not very happy and I never have a lot of energy.

2 At the weekend ...
a I sometimes get up before 9 a.m.
b I always get up before 9 a.m.
c I hardly ever get up before 9 a.m.

3 When I go to a party ...
a I always stay to the end.
b I sometimes stay to the end.
c I never stay to the end.

4 When there's a good film on TV late at night ...
a I always watch it to the end.
b I usually record it and go to bed.
c I often watch the beginning but I never see the end.

5 When I see friends at the weekend ...
a I usually see them in the afternoon.
b I sometimes have coffee with them in the morning.
c I hardly ever see them before 9 p.m.

6 When a friend phones me before 8 a.m. ...
a I'm always happy to talk to him/her.
b I'm sometimes happy to talk to him/her.
c I never answer the phone.

HELP WITH GRAMMAR
Subject and object pronouns

6 **a** Look at the words in pink and blue in these sentences. Which are subject pronouns? Which are object pronouns?

I usually see them in the afternoon.

We hardly ever see him in the week.

b Look at questions 4–6 in the questionnaire. Fill in the table with the object pronouns in blue.

subject pronouns	object pronouns
I	me
you	you
he	
she	
it	
we	us
they	

c Check in GRAMMAR 3.5 > p134.

7 **a** Choose the correct words.

1 Lauren's my sister and I /me see she/her every Sunday.

2 Ian and I phone Eve a lot, but she/her never phones we/us.

3 My name's Zachariah, but my friends always call I/me Zak.

4 Alexander's our son and we/us see he/him every weekend.

5 Rob and Andy are my cousins, but I/me hardly ever talk to they/them.

b Work in pairs. Compare answers. Underline the object pronouns. Who do they refer to?

1 *her → Lauren*

8 **a** Write two things you: always, usually, sometimes, hardly ever do in the morning.

always – get up early, have coffee

b Work in new pairs. Compare answers. Are any the same?

I always get up early in the morning.

Me too.

HELP WITH PRONUNCIATION
How we say *th*

1 **a** CD1▶66 Listen to these sounds and words. Notice the two ways we say *th*.

/θ/	/ð/
fourth thirteenth	the this that
month birthday	these those
think thing	they their
Thursday teeth	with mother
	father brother

b Listen again and practise.

2 **a** CD1▶67 Listen to these sentences. Listen again and practise.

1 Who's that over there with Matthew's father?

2 It's Kathy's thirty-third birthday this Thursday.

3 I think Beth's three brothers are with their mother.

4 That's the sixth or seventh time this month.

5 Thanks for taking those things to Theo's brother.

6 I think those are their father's things.

b Work in pairs. Take turns to say the sentences. Is your partner's pronunciation correct?

c Say one of the sentences for the class.

continue2learn

▶ **Vocabulary, Grammar and Real World**

■ **Extra Practice 3 and Progress Portfolio 3** p117

■ **Language Summary 3** p132

■ **3A–D** Workbook p15

■ **Self-study DVD-ROM 3** with Review Video

▶ **Reading and Writing**

■ **Portfolio 3** All about me Workbook p68
  Reading learner profiles
  Writing connecting words (1): *and, but, because;* a learner profile

Vocabulary and Speaking
Free time activities (2)

1 **a** Tick the phrases you know. Then do the exercise in VOCABULARY 4.1 ▶ p135.

> take photos   go to the gym
> watch sport on TV   play video games
> play tennis   read books or magazines
> go cycling   go swimming   go running
> go clubbing   listen to music
> listen to the radio

TIP • We can say *play video games* or *play computer games*.

b Work in pairs. Ask and answer questions about the free time activities in **1a**.

> Do you watch sport on TV?

> No, never.

> Yes, every weekend.

Listening and Speaking

2 **a** Before you read and listen, check these words with your teacher.

> an observatory   stars   the weather
> a holiday   hot   rain

b Read the email and look at the photo. Where is Trevor? Who is Polly, do you think?

c CD1 ▶ 68 Listen to Polly and her friend, Lorna. Choose the correct answers.

1 Trevor is in *Argentina/Chile*.
2 Trevor and Polly *are/aren't* married.
3 Trevor's got *three/four* weeks' holiday.
4 The hotel *is/isn't* very good.

3 **a** Work in pairs. What does Trevor do in his free time, do you think? Choose six activities from **1a**.

b CD1 ▶ 69 Listen to the rest of Polly and Lorna's conversation. Are your guesses correct?

• We usually link consonant (*b, c, d, f,* etc.) sounds at the end of a word with vowel (*a, e, i, o, u*) sounds at the beginning of the next word.

4 **a** CD1 ▶ 70 Listen and notice the linking.

YOU EXPECT TO HEAR	YOU USUALLY HEAR
And all of	And‿all‿of
the people are nice	the people‿are nice
And all of the people are nice.	And‿all‿of the people‿are nice.

b Look at Audio Script CD1 ▶ 69 p158. Listen again and notice the linking in Polly's part of the conversation.

5 **a** Look at these sentences. Then complete the rules.

*He **plays** video games.*
*He **doesn't like** the weather.*
*He **watches** lots of DVDs.*
*She **doesn't talk** to him very often.*

• In positive sentences with *he, she* and *it* we add _____ or _____ to the infinitive.

• In negative sentences with *he, she* and *it* we use _____ + infinitive.

TIP • *have* is irregular: *he/she/it **has** … : He **has** tennis lessons every week.*

b Check in GRAMMAR 4.1 ▶ p137.

To: polly.carr@gomail.co.uk

Hi Polly

Here's a photo of Cerro Paranal observatory this evening. Isn't it beautiful? What a great place to work. The only problem is – you're not here!

Lots of love
Trevor

6 **a** Check the spelling rules in GRAMMAR 4.2 p137. Then write the *he/she/it* forms of these verbs.

watch	play	go	write	phone	get
finish	have	study	start	do	live

b CD1 ▶71 PRONUNCIATION Listen and practise the infinitives and the *he/she/it* forms of the verbs in **6a**. Which have the sound /ɪz/ at the end?

watch, watches /ɪz/

7 Fill in the gaps with the correct form of the verbs in brackets.

Lorna and Polly are both sales assistants in London, but they
¹ *don't work* (not work) in the same shop. Polly ² _____ (work) in a shoe shop and Lorna ³ _____ (work) in a bookshop. In their free time they ⁴ _____ (read) a lot. Lorna ⁵ _____ (not like) sport, but Polly ⁶ _____ (play) tennis a lot and she ⁷ _____ (watch) sport on TV. At the weekend Lorna ⁸ _____ (not stay) in London. She ⁹ _____ (go) to see her parents in Bath. Polly ¹⁰ _____ (not visit) her parents very often because they ¹¹ _____ (not live) in England.

Get ready ... Get it right!

8 **a** Choose a partner, but don't talk to him/her. Look at the words/phrases in the box. Guess what your partner does or doesn't do in his/her free time. Complete the sentences with the positive or negative form of the verbs in brackets.

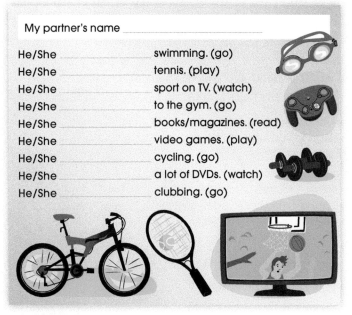

My partner's name _____

He/She	_____	swimming. (go)
He/She	_____	tennis. (play)
He/She	_____	sport on TV. (watch)
He/She	_____	to the gym. (go)
He/She	_____	books/magazines. (read)
He/She	_____	video games. (play)
He/She	_____	cycling. (go)
He/She	_____	a lot of DVDs. (watch)
He/She	_____	clubbing. (go)

b Make questions with *you* for each sentence in the box.

Do you go swimming?

9 **a** Work with your partner. Take turns to ask your questions. How many of your guesses are correct?

Do you go swimming? — Yes, I do. — No, I don't.

Yes, sometimes.

b Tell another student about your partner.

Alex doesn't go swimming, but she plays tennis a lot.

Vocabulary and Speaking
Things you like and don't like

1 Work in pairs. Which of these words/phrases do you know? Then do the exercise in **VOCABULARY 4.2** ▸ **p135**.

> reading   football   travelling   cats
> shopping for clothes   video games
> animals   dancing   cooking
> dance music   rock music   jazz
> Italian food   Chinese food   fast food

2 Put these phrases in order 1–7.

> I love … *1*   I hate … *7*   I like …
> … is/are OK.   I don't like …
> I really like …   I quite like …

HELP WITH VOCABULARY
Verb+*ing*

3 **a** With the phrases in **2** we can use verb+*ing* or a noun. Look at these sentences.
I love ***reading.*** (verb+*ing*)
I like ***books.*** (noun)

b Find all the verb+*ing* words in **1**.

TIP • We use ***enjoy*** + verb+*ing* to say we like doing something: *I enjoy travelling.*

VOCABULARY 4.4 ▸ **p135**

4 Work in pairs. Talk about the things in **1** and your own ideas. Do you like the same things?

> I really like video games.

> Me too./I don't. I hate them.

> Do you like dance music?

> Yes, I love it./It's OK./No, not really.

PRESENTER Hello and welcome to *First Date!*. Tonight you choose a date for Mark Skipper. Mark is 28 years old and he's a teacher. In his free time he watches TV and plays video games. He also goes to the cinema a lot and he plays football and tennis every weekend. He loves rock music and Chinese food, but he hates shopping for clothes! He also likes animals – he's got a dog and three cats. So, Mark – who do you want to ask about first?

Kim

Susie

Jo

MARK Er, Kim, please.

PRESENTER OK. Remember, you can only ask six questions.

Reading, Listening and Speaking

5 **CD1 72** Read and listen to the TV game show, *First Date!*. Find four things Mark likes and one thing he doesn't like.

6 **a** Match Mark's questions about Kim to the presenter's answers.

1 What does she do in her free time?
2 Does she watch TV a lot?
3 Does she like films?
4 What music does she like?
5 Does she like animals?
6 And what does she do?

a Yes, she does. She's got two dogs.
b Yes, she goes to the cinema every Saturday evening.
c She loves dance music, but she doesn't like rock music.
d She plays tennis and she eats out a lot. She loves Italian food.
e No, she doesn't. She hates watching TV!
f She's a vet.

b **CD1 73** Listen and check.

7 a Look at **6a**. Then fill in the gaps with *does* or *doesn't*.

QUESTIONS	SHORT ANSWERS
1 _____ she **like** animals?	Yes, she _____ .
2 _____ she **watch** TV a lot?	No, she _____ .
3 What _____ she **do** in her free time?	

b Look at the table. Notice the word order in questions. Then write questions 3 and 4 from **6a** in the table.

question word	auxiliary	subject	infinitive	
What	does	she	do	in her free time?
	Does	she	watch	TV a lot?

c Check in GRAMMAR 4.3 ▸ p137. Then read GRAMMAR 4.4 ▸ p137.

8 a Write questions with *she*.

1 What / do? *What does she do?*
2 / like rock music?
3 What food / like?
4 / like sport?
5 / have any animals?
6 What / do on Saturday evenings?

b CD1▸74 PRONUNCIATION Listen and check. Listen again and practise. Copy the stress.

What does she do?

c Work in pairs. Ask and answer the questions in **8a** about Kim. Find her answers in **6a**.

9 a Work in pairs. Student A, read about Jo on p105. Student B, read about Susie on p110. Find the answers to the questions in **8a**.

b Work with your partner. Ask and answer the questions in **8a** about Jo or Susie.

c Tell your partner three more things about Jo or Susie.

10 a Work in groups. Which woman do you want to choose for Mark's first date – Kim, Jo or Susie? Why?

b Tell the class which woman your group wants for Mark's first date and why. The class must agree on one person!

c Read about Mark's date with the woman the class chose. (Kim p105, Jo p110, Susie p114). Answer these questions.

1 Does Mark like her? Why?/Why not?
2 Does she like Mark? Why?/Why not?
3 Do they want to see each other again?

Get ready ... Get it right!

11 a Work in pairs, but don't talk to your partner. Choose a friend to introduce to your partner. Tick the things in the box that your friend does or likes.

I've got a friend for you!

My friend's name: _____

☐ watches TV a lot
☐ likes travelling/cooking/clubbing
☐ plays tennis/football
☐ likes shopping for clothes
☐ goes to the cinema a lot
☐ likes cats/dogs/animals
☐ reads a lot of books
☐ likes rock music/dance music/jazz
☐ eats out a lot
☐ likes Chinese/Italian/fast food

b Choose eight things you do or like from the box. Make questions with *he* or *she*.

Does he/she watch TV a lot?

Does he/she like Italian food?

12 a Work with your partner. Ask and answer questions about your friends. First, ask about the friend's name, age, job and where he or she lives. Then ask your questions from **11b**.

b Do you and your partner's friend do or like the same things? Tell another student.

> We both eat out a lot.

> He likes rock music, but I don't.

The Sun Café

Pizzas	Margherita	£8.50
	Neapolitan	£9.25
Burgers	Burger and chips	£8.75
	Cheeseburger and chips	£9.50
Salads	Tuna	£9.50
	Chicken	£10.25
	Mixed	£4.50
Sandwiches	Egg mayonnaise	£5.75
	Cheese and tomato	£6.25
Desserts	Apple pie with cream	£5.25
	Fruit salad	£4.75
	Vanilla, chocolate or strawberry ice cream	£3.25
Drinks	Red/White wine (Glass)	£4.75
	(Bottle)	£14.50
	Bottle of beer	£3.75
	Bottle of mineral water (still or sparkling)	£2.75
	Tea or coffee	£2.50

See you at the Sun Café!

1 Work in groups. Discuss these questions.

1 When do you usually eat out?
2 What's your favourite café or restaurant?
3 Is it cheap or expensive?
4 What do you usually eat there?

2 **a** Work in pairs. Match photos 1–13 to food and drink on the menu. Check in **VOCABULARY 4.5** p136.

b Work in pairs. Take turns to point to photos 1–13 and test your partner.

> What's number 1?

> A cheese and tomato sandwich.

3 Work in pairs. Take turns to choose something to eat and drink from the menu. Ask your partner questions with *How much ... ?*

> How much is a tuna salad and a bottle of mineral water?

> Twelve pounds twenty-five.

HELP WITH LISTENING *Would you like ... ?*

4 **a** CD1 ▶ 75 We use *Would you like ... ?* for offers. Listen and notice how we say *would you* in questions.

YOU EXPECT TO HEAR
would you /wʊd juː/
Would you /wʊd juː/ like to order now?

YOU USUALLY HEAR
would you /wʊdʒə/
Would you /wʊdʒə/ like to order now?

b CD1 ▶ 76 Listen and put these questions in the order you hear them.

a Would you like tea or coffee?   **c** Would you like a dessert?
b Would you like anything else?   **d** What would you like to drink?

5 **a** VIDEO ▶ 4 CD1 ▶ 77 Close your books. Watch or listen to Paul and Clare at the Sun Café. What do they order?

b Work in pairs. Compare answers.

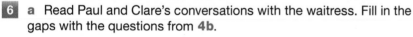
Paul   Clare

REAL WORLD
Requests and offers

7 **a** Look at sentences 1–3. Which sentences are requests (we want something)? Which sentence is an offer (we want to give something or help someone)?

1 **Would you like** to order now?

2 **I'd / We'd like** a bottle of mineral water, please.

3 **Can I / we have** the bill, please?

b Complete the rules with the phrases in bold in **7a**.

● We use _____ and _____ for requests.

● We use _____ for offers.

c Look at the conversation in **6a** again. Find four more requests.

REAL WORLD 4.1 ▶ p137

8 **a** CD1 ▶78 Listen to the sentences in **7a**. Notice the stress and polite intonation.

Would you like to order now?

b CD1 ▶79 **PRONUNCIATION** Listen and practise the offers and requests in the conversation in **6a**. Copy the stress and polite intonation.

9 **a** Work in groups of three. Decide who is the waiter/waitress and who are the customers. Practise the conversation in **6a** until you remember it.

b Close your book. Practise the conversation again.

10 **a** Work in the same groups. Look at the menu. Write a new conversation between a waiter/waitress and two customers.

b Swap conversations with another group. Correct any mistakes.

c Practise the new conversation with your partner. Then role-play it for the other group.

6 **a** Read Paul and Clare's conversations with the waitress. Fill in the gaps with the questions from **4b**.

WAITRESS Would you like to order now?
CLARE Yes, I'd like the chicken salad, please.
PAUL Can I have the cheeseburger and chips, please?
WAITRESS ¹ _____ ?
CLARE We'd like a bottle of mineral water, please.
WAITRESS Still or sparkling?
CLARE Sparkling, please.
WAITRESS ² _____ ?
PAUL No, that's all, thanks.

WAITRESS ³ _____ ?
CLARE Yes, I'd like the fruit salad, please.
PAUL And can I have the apple pie with cream?
WAITRESS Certainly.

WAITRESS ⁴ _____ ?
CLARE Not for me, thank you.
PAUL No, thank you. Can we have the bill, please?
WAITRESS Yes, of course.

b VIDEO ▶4 CD1 ▶77 Watch or listen again. Check your answers.

VOCABULARY 4D AND SKILLS ▶ Breakfast time

Vocabulary food and drink (2);
countable and uncountable nouns
Skills listening: a conversation

QUICK REVIEW Food and drink Work in pairs. What's on the Sun Café menu? Work with another pair. Which pair has the most things? Check the menu on p36.

1 Tick the food and drink you know. Then do the exercise in VOCABULARY 4.6 ▶ p136.

> biscuits   milk   an apple   rice   yogurt
> sugar   toast   bread   fish   eggs   coffee
> sausages   soup   cheese   a banana
> orange juice   a croissant   tea   jam   meat
> fruit   cereal   olives   tomatoes   vegetables

2 Which of the things in **1** do you usually have for breakfast? Is this typical for your country? Compare answers in groups.

3 **a** What do you think people in Japan, France and Turkey have for breakfast? Work in pairs and make three lists. Use words from **1**.

b CD1▶80 Listen to a chef and his assistant, Dylan, at a language school in the UK. Tick the food and drink on your lists that they talk about.

c Listen again. Complete your lists of the three breakfast menus.

4 **a** Look at the pictures in the table. Then choose the correct words.

1 We *can/can't* count biscuits and apples.
2 We *can/can't* count milk and rice.

COUNTABLE NOUNS		UNCOUNTABLE NOUNS

singular	plural		
a biscuit	*biscuits*	*milk*	*rice*
an apple	*apples*		

b Write the words from **1** in the table. Write the singular and plural if possible.

HELP WITH VOCABULARY
Countable and uncountable nouns

5 **a** Look at the table in **4a**. Choose the correct words in these rules.

COUNTABLE NOUNS

● Countable nouns *have/don't have* a plural form.

● We *use/don't use* **a** or **an** with singular countable nouns.

● We *use/don't use* **a** or **an** with plural countable nouns.

UNCOUNTABLE NOUNS

● Uncountable nouns *are/aren't* usually plural.

● We *use/don't use* **a** or **an** with uncountable nouns.

b Check in VOCABULARY 4.7 ▶ p136.

6 Choose the correct answer: *a*, *an* or – (no article).

1 Sue never has *a*/– milk in her tea.
2 I have *an*/– egg for breakfast every day.
3 Do you want *a*/– biscuit?
4 I love *a*/– cheese sandwiches.
5 Ted usually has *a*/– soup for lunch.
6 Would you like *a*/– banana?
7 Do you eat *a*/– fruit?

7 **a** Fill in the gaps with *a*, *an* or – .

1 I often have _____ rice with my main meal.
2 My friends and I sometimes go out for _____ burger.
3 I always have _____ toast and jam for breakfast.
4 I never have _____ sugar in coffee.
5 I like _____ olives in my salad.
6 I have _____ apple every day.
7 I often have _____ sandwich for lunch.
8 I never eat _____ meat.

b Make the sentences in **7a** true for you. Change the underlined words if necessary.

I often have chips with my main meal.

c Work in pairs. Compare sentences. Are any the same?

8 Work in groups. Tell the other students which food and drink you like/don't like.

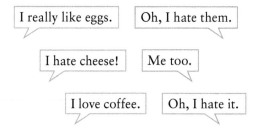

I really like eggs.   Oh, I hate them.

I hate cheese!   Me too.

I love coffee.   Oh, I hate it.

9 **a** Imagine your perfect breakfast. Answer these questions.

1 Where are you?
2 What time is it?
3 Who are you with?
4 What do you have for breakfast?
5 What do you do after breakfast?

b Work in groups. Tell the other students about your perfect breakfast.

HELP WITH PRONUNCIATION
/ʃ/, /tʃ/ and /dʒ/

1 CD1▶81 Listen to the sounds and words. Listen again and practise.

1 /ʃ/ **sh**opping fini**sh** Turki**sh**
2 /tʃ/ **ch**eap wa**tch** **ch**ildren
3 /dʒ/ **G**ermany **J**apan sausa**g**es

2 **a** Work in pairs. Match the letters in bold in these words to sounds 1–3 in **1**.

| English *1* che**ese** **j**am **ch**icken |
| vegetables sandwi**ch** musi**c**ian en**g**ineer |
| tea**ch**er Ru**ss**ia **j**azz nationality |

b CD1▶82 Listen and check. Listen again and practise.

3 **a** CD1▶83 Listen to these sentences. Listen again and practise.

1 My Russian teacher loves jazz.
2 George eats a lot of jam sandwiches.
3 Jane loves chocolate and Turkish coffee.
4 Janet's got a cheap Japanese watch.
5 Joe often has chicken and vegetables.
6 Roger likes Spanish sausages, French cheese and German beer.

b Work in pairs. Take turns to say the sentences. Is your partner's pronunciation correct?

continue2learn

▶ **Vocabulary, Grammar and Real World**

■ **Extra Practice 4 and Progress Portfolio 4** p118
■ **Language Summary 4** p135
■ **4A–D** Workbook p20
■ **Self-study DVD-ROM 4** with Review Video

face2face Elementary DVD-ROM
DVD-ROM

▶ **Reading and Writing**

■ **Portfolio 4** Going out Workbook p70
Reading restaurant adverts
Writing messages (1): an email

QUICK REVIEW Food and drink Work in pairs. Write all the words for food and drink you know. Compare answers with another pair. Which pair has more words? Which words are countable/uncountable?

Vocabulary Adjectives (2)

1 a Work in pairs. Which of these adjectives do you know? Then do the exercise in VOCABULARY 5.1 p138.

hot	cold
noisy	quiet
well	ill
short	tall
lucky	unlucky
different	the same
happy	unhappy
boring	interesting
friendly	unfriendly
terrible/awful	fantastic/amazing/wonderful

b Work in pairs. Test your partner on the opposites.

happy   unhappy

Listening and Reading

2 a Look at photo A. Where are the people? What's their relationship, do you think?

b CD2 1 Listen and read. Who is talking? How old is he?

I live in Bristol with my parents and my sister. It was my thirteenth birthday yesterday and there was a big party at our house. About thirty people were here, and we were lucky because it was a very hot day. I was happy because my granddad was here from Liverpool. There were only two things wrong. My best friend Robert wasn't here because he was ill. And my two brothers weren't here because they're in the USA. But it was a fantastic party!

c Read about the party again. Which of these things are <u>not</u> in the text?

- where the family lives
- the weather
- people at the party
- people not at the party
- food and drink
- birthday presents

A   Albert   Matt   Jason

HELP WITH GRAMMAR
Past Simple (1): *be* (positive and negative)

3 a Look at the text in **2b** again. Underline all the examples of *was*, *wasn't*, *were* and *weren't*.

b Fill in the gaps with *was*, *wasn't*, *were* and *weren't*.

POSITIVE (+)	NEGATIVE (−)
I was	I _____ (= was not)
you/we/they _____	you/we/they _____ (= were not)
he/she/it _____	he/she/it _____

c Check in GRAMMAR 5.1 p139.

4 Read about Matt's thirteenth birthday party. Choose the correct words.

I ¹(*was*)/*were* born in Liverpool in 1974 and I ²*was/were* thirteen in 1987. Our house ³*wasn't/weren't* very big, so my party ⁴*was/were* at my grandparents' house. The house ⁵*was/were* cold and the food ⁶*wasn't/weren't* very nice. Only about twelve people ⁷*was/were* at the party and there ⁸*wasn't/weren't* any girls my age. So the party ⁹*was/were* a bit boring.

B

Listening and Speaking

5 **a** `CD2` 2 Look at photo B. Listen to Jason ask his grandfather, Albert, about his thirteenth birthday party. Where was he? Why was his birthday a special day?

b Listen again and answer the questions.

1 When was Albert's 13th birthday?
2 Where was the party?
3 Were his friends there?
4 Was the food good?
5 Where were his grandparents?

HELP WITH LISTENING
Weak forms (2): *was* and *were*

6 **a** `CD2` 3 Listen and notice the weak forms of *was* and *were*.

I was /wəz/ in Liverpool with my parents.
All my friends were /wə/ there.
Was /wəz/ the food good?
Were /wə/ your grandparents there?

b Look at Audio Script `CD2` 2 p159. Listen again and notice the weak forms of *was* and *were* in pink.

HELP WITH GRAMMAR Past Simple (1): *be* (questions and short answers)

7 **a** Look at the table. Notice the word order. Then write questions 2, 4 and 5 from **5b** in the table.

question word	*was/were*	subject	
When	was	Albert's	13th birthday?
	Were	his friends	there?

b Fill in the gaps in these short answers with *was*, *were*, *wasn't* or *weren't*.

Yes, I/he/she/it _____ .   No, I/he/she/it _____ .
Yes, you/we/they _____ .   No, you/we/they _____ .

c Fill in the gaps with *was* or *were*.

1 A When _____ you born?
  B I _____ born in 1940.
2 A Where _____ Matt born?
  B He _____ born in Liverpool.

d Check in `GRAMMAR 5.2` p139.

8 `CD2` 4 `PRONUNCIATION` Listen and practise. Copy the stress and weak forms.

I was /wəz/ in Liverpool with my parents.

9 **a** Work in pairs. How do we say these years?

> 1835   1900   1990   2000   2005   2018

b `CD2` 5 `PRONUNCIATION` Listen and check. Listen again and practise.

c Write the names of five people in your family. Then work in pairs. Swap papers. Ask your partner when and where the people were born.

> When was Miguel born?   In 1986.

10 **a** Make questions with *you*.

1 / at work yesterday?   *Were you at work yesterday?*
2 Where / last night?
3 / at home yesterday afternoon?
4 Where / on your last birthday?
5 Where / last New Year's Eve?

b Work in new pairs. Ask and answer the questions. Give more information if possible.

Get ready ... Get it right!

11 Work in pairs. Student A p106. Student B p111.

QUICK REVIEW Past Simple (1): *be* Write six times of the day. Work in pairs. Ask your partner where he/she was at these times yesterday: *Where were you at six in the evening?*

Vocabulary
Life events

1 **a** Work in pairs. Fill in the gaps in the phrases with these verbs. Check in VOCABULARY 5.3 ▸ p138.

~~leave~~ make become meet get

1 *leave* school/university
2 _____ my husband/my wife
3 _____ married/divorced
4 _____ a film/a lot of money
5 _____ a film director/famous

~~have~~ write study win move

6 *have* children/a dream
7 _____ house/to a different country
8 _____ English/physics
9 _____ a book/a letter
10 _____ an Oscar/the lottery

b Work in pairs. Take turns to test your partner on the phrases.

> married   get married

Speaking, Reading and Listening

2 Work in groups. Look at posters A–D. What do you know about these films? What do you know about the director James Cameron?

3 **a** Check these words with your teacher.

> a script   a robot   successful
> diving   3D   a billion

b Read the article about James Cameron's life. Fill in the gaps with these dates and numbers.

> 1971   twelve   1999   two
> August 16th   1986 $2 billion

c Work in pairs. Compare answers.

d CD2 6 Listen and check your answers.

CAMERON'S WORLD

James Cameron was born in Ontario, Canada, on ª_____ 1954. His family moved to the USA in ᵇ_____ . James went to California State University and studied physics and English. He left university after only ᶜ_____ years because he wanted to become a film director. He worked as a bus driver in the day and wrote film scripts at night. James's first job as a director was on a film called *Piranha 2*. One night after filming he had a bad dream about a robot from the future. The next day James started writing the script of *The Terminator*. The film was very successful and Cameron became famous all around the world.

He then made *Aliens* in ᵈ_____ , *Terminator 2* in 1991 and *Titanic* in 1997. At that time James loved diving, and he visited the Titanic ᵉ_____ times before he started making the film. *Titanic* made ᶠ_____ and won eleven Oscars. His next film was the first *Avatar* movie in 2009, which he made in 3D.

James met Linda Hamilton – Sarah Connor in the *Terminator* films – in 1984 and she became his fourth wife in 1997. They had one daughter, but they got divorced in ᵍ_____ . A year later he married actress Suzy Amis, who was in *Titanic*. They have two daughters and a son.

HELP WITH GRAMMAR
Past Simple (2): regular and irregular verbs (positive)

4 **a** Look at the regular Past Simple forms in blue in the article. Then answer these questions.

1 How do we make the Past Simple of regular verbs?
2 What do we do when the verb ends in *-e* (*move, love*, etc.)?
3 What do we do when the verb ends in *-y* (*study, marry*, etc.)?

b Look at the irregular Past Simple forms in pink in the article. Match them to verbs 1–9.

1 become _____   4 have _____   7 meet _____
2 get _____   5 leave _____   8 win _____
3 go _____   6 make _____   9 write _____

TIP • The Past Simple is the same for all subjects (*I, you, he, she, it, we, they*).

c Check in GRAMMAR 5.3 ▸ p139 and in the Irregular Verb List, p167.

5 a CD2 ▶7 PRONUNCIATION Listen and practise the regular verbs in the article and their Past Simple forms. Which end with the sound /ɪd/?

b CD2 ▶8 PRONUNCIATION Listen and practise the irregular verbs in **4b** and their Past Simple forms.

HELP WITH LISTENING
Present Simple or Past Simple

6 a CD2 ▶9 Listen to these sentences. Notice the difference between the Present Simple and the Past Simple.

1 I **love** all his films. I **loved** all his films.
2 They **live** in L.A. They **lived** in L.A.

b CD2 ▶10 Listen to six pairs of sentences. Which do you hear <u>first</u>, the Present Simple or the Past Simple?

1 Present Simple

7 Fill in the gaps with the Past Simple of these verbs.

~~love~~	marry	write	win	be	get	start	make

1 James Cameron _loved_ films when he _____ a child.
2 He _____ the film director Kathryn Bigelow in 1989, but they _____ divorced in 1991.
3 He _____ the script for the second *Rambo* film.
4 He _____ a film called *True Lies* in 1994.
5 His film *Aliens* _____ two Oscars.
6 He _____ writing the script for *Avatar* in 1995.

8 a Cover the article. Choose the correct answers.

1 What did James study at university?
   a Physics.   **b** English.   **c** Physics and English.
2 When did he make *Terminator 2*?
   a In 1986.   **b** In 1991.   **c** In 1999.
3 Which film did he make in 3D in 2009?
   a *Aliens*   **b** *Titanic*   **c** *Avatar*
4 Who did he marry in 1997?
   a Sarah Connor.   **b** Suzy Amis.   **c** Linda Hamilton.

b Look at the article. Check your answers.

HELP WITH GRAMMAR
Past Simple (2): *Wh-* questions

9 a Look at the table. Notice the word order in questions. Then write questions 3 and 4 from **8a** in the table.

question word	auxiliary	subject	infinitive	
What	did	James	study	at university?
When	did	he	make	*Terminator 2*?

b Check in GRAMMAR 5.4 ▶ p139.

10 a Make questions with these words.

1 yesterday / did / you / What / do ?
2 go on holiday / you / did / last year / Where ?
3 What / you / last weekend / do / did ?
4 see / last month / How many films / you / did ?
5 meet / you / your best friend / did / Where ?

b CD2 ▶11 PRONUNCIATION Listen and check. Notice how we say *did you* /dɪdʒə/. Listen again and practise.

Whàt did you /dɪdʒə/ dò yèsterday?

c Work in pairs. Ask and answer the questions in **10a**.

Get ready ... Get it right!

11 Work in pairs. Look at p114.

REAL WORLD 5C

Four weekends

Real World showing interest;
asking follow-up questions
Vocabulary weekend activities

QUICK REVIEW Past Simple Write six
verbs you know. Work in pairs. Say the
verb to your partner. He/She says a
sentence with the Past Simple form:
A *go* B *I went to England last year.*

Weekend activities

1 a Work in pairs. Look at phrases 1–8.
Then fill in the gaps with these words/
phrases. Check in VOCABULARY 5.4 p138.

> a run   for a couple of days
> the house   a bad cold   a report
> at home all weekend   your homework
> your parents' house for lunch

1 **go for** — a walk
a run

2 **clean** — the car
____

3 **do** — the washing
____

4 **write** — an email
____

5 **go away** — for the weekend
____

6 **have** — a great time
____

7 **go to** — a party
____

8 **stay** — with friends
____

b What are the Past Simple forms
of the verbs in **1a**?

2 a Think of five things you did last
weekend. Use phrases from **1a** or
your own ideas.

b Work in pairs. Ask your partner
what he or she did last weekend.
Find three things you both did.

> What did you do last weekend?
> I went for a walk on Sunday.
> Me too.

Emily

Tim

A

To: Clive Roberts

Hi Clive

Just a note to say I'm sorry I wasn't at the
party. I was ill all weekend. I think it was
because I worked every evening last week!

B goldfish

Had a quiet weekend. Stayed in and watched
TV on Saturday. Last night I went to the
cinema to see *A Day in the Life*.

10th June at 07.46 Like Comment Share

How was your weekend?

3 a VIDEO 5 CD2 12 Look at the photos and read A–D. Then watch or
listen to two conversations and match the people to A–D.

b Watch or listen again. Are these sentences true (T) or false (F)?

CONVERSATION 1
1 Tim had a terrible weekend. *T*
2 Emily did the washing on Saturday.
3 She went to the theatre.
4 She didn't like the film.

CONVERSATION 2
5 Rachel went to Madrid with a friend.
6 She stayed in a hotel.
7 Simon had an interesting weekend.
8 He finished the report on Sunday
evening.

44

Rachel   Simon

C
Things to do
• go shopping ✓
• clean the car ✓
• check emails ✓
• go to gym ✓
• write report ✓

D
📶 80   9.17am
All Contacts   Edit

Hi Pablo and Marta!
It was great to go away
for the weekend. We had
a wonderful time with you
in Madrid. Thanks again!

REAL WORLD Showing interest

4 **a** CD2 ▶13 Listen to parts of the conversations in **3b** again. Match sentences 1–8 to responses a–h.

1 I was ill all weekend.   a Oh, right.
2 I had a really bad cold.   b Wow!
3 I stayed at home on Saturday.   c Oh, dear.
4 I went to the cinema.   d What a shame.
5 I went away for the weekend – to Spain!   e Really?
6 We went to Madrid. It was wonderful!   f You're joking!
7 I worked all Sunday.   g Oh, nice.
8 It took me ten hours.   h Oh, great!

b Fill in the table with responses a–h.

I'm happy for you.	I'm sorry for you.	I'm surprised.	I'm not surprised.
			Oh, right.

c Check in REAL WORLD 5.1 ▶ p139.

5 CD2 ▶14 **PRONUNCIATION** Listen and practise the responses in **4b**. Copy the intonation.

REAL WORLD
Asking follow-up questions

6 **a** Look at these follow-up questions from the conversations in **3b**. Fill in the gaps with *did*, *was* or *are*.

1 What _____ wrong?
2 _____ you OK now?
3 What _____ you do?
4 What _____ you see?
5 What *was* it like?
6 Where _____ you go?
7 Who _____ you go with?
8 Where _____ you stay?

b Which of the questions in **6a** can you ask someone who:

a was ill at the weekend?
b stayed at home?
c went to the cinema?
d went away for the weekend?

c Check in REAL WORLD 5.2 ▶ p139.

7 **a** Work in pairs. Look at VIDEO ▶5 CD2 ▶12 p159. Choose one of the conversations. Underline all the responses from **4a** and follow-up questions from **6a**.

b Practise the conversation with your partner.

8 **a** Make notes on what you did at these times.

● last weekend
● last week
● yesterday
● before you came to this lesson
● on Friday evening

b Work in new pairs. Ask and answer questions about the times in **8a**. Use the follow-up questions from **6a**. How long can you continue each conversation?

What did you do last weekend?

Well, I went to a party on Saturday.

Oh, nice. What was it like?

It was great!

c Tell the class three things about your partner.

VOCABULARY
5D AND SKILLS ▷ Competitions

Vocabulary adjectives (3); adjectives
with *very, really, quite, too*
Skills reading: a magazine article

QUICK REVIEW Past Simple Work in pairs. Take turns to tell your partner five things you did last week: **A** *I went to a concert on Saturday.* Ask follow-up questions to get more information: **B** *What was it like?*

1 a Work in pairs. Which of these adjectives do you know? Then do the exercise in **VOCABULARY 5.5** ▷ p138.

> bored   crowded   busy   comfortable
> dirty   rich   dangerous   clean
> poor   excited   safe   empty

b Put the words in **1a** into groups a–c:

a adjectives for people *bored*

b adjectives for places *crowded*

c adjectives for places and people *busy*

c Work in pairs. Compare answers. Which words in **1a** are opposites?

2 a Before you read, check these words/phrases with your teacher.

> enter a competition   win a prize
> a castle   a queue   a receptionist

b Work in pairs. Discuss these questions.

1 Do you think you're a lucky person? Why?/Why not?

2 Do you (or people you know) enter competitions in magazines or on the internet?

3 What prizes do people win in competitions?

4 What prize would you like to win?

c Look at the magazine article. Read the first paragraph only. What is the article about?

3 a Work in pairs. Student A, read about Bruce. Student B, read about Sally. Answer these questions.

1 What did he/she win?

2 Who did he/she go with?

3 Did he/she like the hotel?

4 What did they do on Saturday?

5 Where did they have dinner?

6 Was the food good?

7 What did Bruce/Craig do on Sunday?

b Work with your partner and ask the questions. Student A, ask about Sally. Student B, ask about Bruce. Give more information if possible.

c Read your partner's text. Check his/her answers.

Winners and Losers

A lot of people enter competitions every year and 99% of them never win anything. But what about the winners? Do they always enjoy their prizes? We talked to two people with very different experiences.

BRUCE I won a weekend for two in Kraków, in Poland. I went with my girlfriend, Olivia, and we stayed in a very nice hotel by the river. The rooms were really comfortable and the people were very friendly. On Saturday we went for a walk in the Old Town. It was quite crowded, but all the shops and buildings were really interesting. We wanted to visit Wawel Castle, but the queues were quite long, so we had lunch instead. In the evening we went back to the hotel and had dinner in the restaurant. It was very busy, but the food was fantastic! Then on Sunday I asked Olivia to marry me – and she said yes! We were very happy when we got home. It was a wonderful weekend in a beautiful city!

SALLY I'm not usually very lucky, but last year I won a weekend for two in Cardiff. I went with my boyfriend, Craig. I was really excited because I love Wales, but the hotel was really awful. It was in a poor part of town and the rooms were very small and quite noisy. On Saturday we didn't leave the hotel because it was too cold. Craig watched sport on TV all day and I was really bored! We had dinner in the hotel, but the restaurant was quite dirty and the food was awful. I went to bed early, but Craig stayed up and talked to the receptionist for hours. She was very young and friendly – too friendly! On Sunday Craig left me and went away with her. It was a terrible weekend!

HELP WITH VOCABULARY
Adjectives with *very, really, quite, too*

4 **a** Look at pictures 1–3 and read the sentences. Which word in bold means 'more than you want'?

It's **quite** big. It's **very/really** big. It's **too** big.

b Complete the rule with *before* and *after*.

● *Very, really, quite* and *too* come _____ the verb *be* and _____ adjectives.

VOCABULARY 5.6 ▶ p138

5 **a** Read the article again and underline all the examples of *very, really, quite, too* + adjective.

b Work in pairs. Compare answers.

6 Choose the correct words.

1 Don't go out on your own at night. It's *quite/(too)* dangerous.
2 He's a famous musician and he's *too/very* rich.
3 Let's go to that new café. It's *really/too* nice.
4 Sorry, sir, you're *quite/too* late. The restaurant is closed.
5 This sofa's *very/too* comfortable.
6 Jill's got a new job and she's *really/too* happy.
7 It's a nice town and the people are *very/too* friendly.
8 You're only 15. You're *quite/too* young to drive.

7 **a** Write the name of a place in the town or city where you are now that is:

1 too expensive or quite cheap
2 really beautiful or really ugly
3 too crowded or quite empty
4 really boring or really interesting
5 too noisy or very quiet
6 very safe or quite dangerous

b Work in groups and compare places. Do you know any of the places the other students talk about? If so, do you agree?

> I think the new coffee shop is very cheap.

> Me too.

> Really? I think it's quite expensive!

HELP WITH PRONUNCIATION
The letter *o*

1 **CD2** ▶ 15 Listen and notice four ways we say the letter *o*. Listen again and practise.

/ɒ/ hot long often /ʌ/ son month mother
/əʊ/ old home phone /ə/ actor police second

2 **a** Work in pairs. Write the words in the table.

coffee sofa tomato wonderful
shopping sometimes mobile computer
open director bottle comfortable

/ɒ/	h**o**t	*coffee*
/əʊ/	**o**ld	
/ʌ/	s**o**n	
/ə/	act**o**r	

b **CD2** ▶ 16 Listen and check. Listen again and practise.

3 Work in pairs. Cover **1** and **2a**. Say these words. Which letter *o* sound is different?

1 tomato actor (sometimes) director
2 phone wonderful mobile old
3 son month bottle comfortable
4 mother often hot shopping
5 police second computer long
6 open home sofa coffee

continue2learn

▶ **Vocabulary, Grammar and Real World**
■ **Extra Practice 5 and Progress Portfolio 5** p119
■ **Language Summary 5** p138
■ **5A–D** Workbook p25
■ **Self-study DVD-ROM 5** with Review Video

▶ **Reading and Writing**
■ **Portfolio 5** A night to remember Workbook p72
  Reading a student's composition
  Writing paragraphs (1); connecting words (2): *after, when* and *then*; a composition

6A ▶ Google it!

Vocabulary the internet
Grammar Past Simple (3): negative,
yes/no questions and short answers

QUICK REVIEW Adjectives with *very, really, quite, too*
Think of three places you went to last year. Work
in pairs. Tell your partner about the places. Use
adjectives with *very, really, quite* and *too*: *I went to
Istanbul last year. It was really beautiful.*

Vocabulary and Speaking
The internet

1 **a** Choose the correct verbs in these sentences
about the internet. Then check in **VOCABULARY 6.1** ▶ **p140**.

1 Do you use /send the internet every day?
2 How many emails do you *go/send* every day?
3 How many emails do you *get/chat* every day?
4 When did you last *chat/read* a blog?
5 Do you *download/go* videos or music onto
your computer?
6 When did you last *go/send* online?
7 Do you *get/have* a favourite website?
8 Do you *send/chat* to your friends online?
9 Which places in your town or city *have/download* WiFi?
10 Which search engine do you usually *write/use*?

b Work in pairs. Ask and answer the questions.
Ask follow-up questions if possible.

Reading and Speaking

2 **a** Before you read, check these words/phrases
with your teacher.

launch	computer science	build (past: built)
a cheque	a bank account	a billionaire

b Read the article about the Google Guys. Match
headings a–d to paragraphs 1–4.

a Starting the business
b How Page and Brin met
c The internet before 1998
d Building a new search engine

c Read the article again. Tick the true sentences.
Correct the false sentences.

            difficult
1 Before 1998 it was ~~easy~~ to find things on the internet. *F*
2 Page and Brin first met in 1997.
3 They had a lot of cheap computers in their room.
4 They built Google when they were students.
5 Google was the first name for their search engine.
6 Page and Brin became billionaires in 2004.

THE Google GUYS

1 What did we do before Google? In the early days of the
internet, search engines weren't very good and it wasn't
easy for people to find the information they wanted. Then
in 1998, Larry Page and Sergey Brin launched the Google
search engine. Suddenly it was easy to find the right
website in seconds.

Larry Page

Sergey Brin

HELP WITH GRAMMAR
Past Simple (3): negative

3 Complete the rules with words from these sentences.

Search engines weren't very good.
They didn't like each other at first.

● To make the Past Simple negative of the verb *be*, we
use *wasn't* or _____ .
● To make the Past Simple negative of all other verbs, we
use _____ + infinitive.

GRAMMAR 6.1 ▶ **p141**

4 **a** Find six more Past Simple negatives in the article.

b Work in pairs. Compare answers.

5 **CD2** 17 **PRONUNCIATION** Listen and practise.
They didn't like each other at first.

2 So how did it all begin? Page and Brin met in 1995 when they started studying computer science at Stanford University in California. They didn't like each other at first, but they became friends when they shared a room together at university.

3 While Page and Brin were at Stanford, they got a lot of cheap computers and started to build a new search engine in their room. At first they called it BackRub, but they weren't happy with the name so they changed it to Google. They didn't finish their course and left Stanford in 1997.

4 Page and Brin wanted to start a business together, but they didn't have any money. At first their families and friends helped them. Then in August 1998 a businessman wrote a cheque to Google Inc for $100,000. But Page and Brin didn't get the money for a month because they didn't have a bank account. Six years later they were billionaires!

6 **a** Tick the sentences that are true for you. Make the other sentences negative.

1 I got lots of emails yesterday.
   I didn't get lots of emails yesterday.
2 I watched a DVD on my computer last Saturday.
3 I used the internet every day last week.
4 I downloaded a lot of music last weekend.
5 I got a new laptop last year.
6 I chatted online with a friend last night.

b Work in pairs. Compare sentences. How many are the same?

Listening and Speaking

7 **a** CD2▶18 Listen to a radio interview with the writer, Wes Clark. Put these people, places and things in the order you hear them.

> Michigan State University   Wes Clark's new book *1*
> Russia   Sergey's mother   Maryland University
> Larry's parents   Sergey's father

b Listen again. Answer the questions.

1 Did Sergey leave Russia in 1978?
2 Did his father teach mathematics?
3 Were Sergey and his father at the same university?
4 Did Larry go to Maryland University?
5 Did his parents teach computer science?
6 Was Larry at the same university as his parents?

HELP WITH GRAMMAR Past Simple (3): *yes/no* questions and short answers

8 Fill in the gaps in these *yes/no* questions and short answers with *did* or *didn't*.

1 **A** *Did* Sergey leave Russia in 1978?
   B Yes, he _____./No, he _____ .
2 **A** _____ his parents teach computer science?
   B Yes, they _____./No, they _____ .

GRAMMAR 6.2▶ p141

9 **a** Make *yes/no* questions with these words.

1 in 1994 / Sergey and Larry / meet / Did ?
   Did Sergey and Larry meet in 1994?
2 they / at first / each other / Did / like ?
3 Sergey / Did / Maryland University / go to ?
4 Larry's parents / teach / mathematics / Did ?
5 study / Sergey / Did / computer science ?
6 launch / Google / in 1999 / Sergey and Larry / Did ?

b CD2▶19 PRONUNCIATION Listen and practise the questions in **9a** and the short answers. Copy the stress.

Did Sergey and Larry meet in 1994?

c Work in pairs. Ask and answer the questions in **9a**.

Get ready … Get it right!

10 Write *yes/no* questions with *you* and these ideas. Use these verbs.

> ~~go~~   play   have   read
> watch (x2)   go to (x2)

1 shopping last weekend?
   Did you go shopping last weekend?
2 a good book last month?
3 sport on TV last weekend?
4 a concert last month?
5 tennis or football last week?
6 a DVD last weekend?
7 the cinema last week?
8 dinner at home last night?

11 **a** Ask other students your questions. Find one person who did each thing. Ask follow-up questions.

b Tell the class two things about the people you talked to.

> Beata went shopping last weekend.
> She bought a new laptop.

6B ▷ Changing technology

Vocabulary mobile phones and TVs;
           past time phrases
Grammar *can/can't*; *could/couldn't*

Vocabulary and Speaking
Mobile phones and TVs

1 **a** Work in pairs. Which of these words/
phrases do you know? Check in
VOCABULARY 6.2 ▷ p140.

> send/get a text   charge your phone   GPS
> a channel   a TV programme   a battery
> an app   turn on   turn off   record

b Work on your own. Put the words/phrases
into three groups: TVs, mobile phones, TVs
and mobile phones.

c Work in pairs. Compare answers. Did you
put the words/phrases in the same groups?

2 **a** Put these past time phrases in order.

twenty minutes ago *1*	in 1986
two years ago	last year
in May 2002	last Monday
in the eighteenth century	yesterday
the day before yesterday	in the nineties

b Fill in the gaps with *ago*, *last* or *in*.

1 I left school four years *ago* .
2 I went to bed quite late _____ Saturday.
3 My parents were born _____ the sixties.
4 My parents got married _____ 1985.
5 I didn't have a holiday _____ year.
6 I started learning English six years _____ .
7 I got my mobile _____ March.
8 I bought my computer two years _____ .

c Tick the sentences in **2b** that are true for
you. Change the time phrases in the other
sentences to make them true for you.

I left school ten years ago.

d Work in pairs. Compare sentences. Are
any the same?

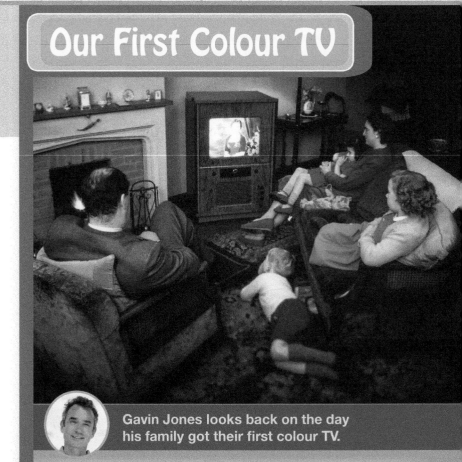

Our First Colour TV

Gavin Jones looks back on the day
his family got their first colour TV.

These days the internet, laptops, mobiles and video games are part
of normal life. My son and daughter can't understand how people
lived without them. But life wasn't always like this. I was a child in the
seventies, when things were very different.

I remember my family's first TV very well. In the seventies you
could only get three channels – and they were in black and white.
Everybody watched live TV all the time because you couldn't record
TV programmes. And you couldn't watch TV all night because there
weren't any programmes after midnight!

Reading and Speaking

3 **a** Before you read, check these words/phrases with
your teacher.

> without   colour   black and white   live TV   explain

b Read the article. How was TV different in the seventies?

c Read the article again. Answer these questions.

1 How many children has Gavin got?
2 When was Gavin a child?
3 When did his family get their first colour TV?
4 What did his family do that evening?
5 What type of TV has Gavin got now?

Then, in June 1974, my life changed for ever. I came home from school and there it was – our family's first colour TV. I was really excited because I *could watch* all my favourite programmes in colour! After dinner my father turned on the TV for the first time and my grandfather took a photo. Then the whole family watched TV together until midnight with biscuits and cups of hot chocolate. It was one of the best evenings of my life – and I've still got the photo!

Of course, now you *can choose* from hundreds of TV channels and watch anything you want at any time of day. You *can watch* TV programmes online and download them onto your mobile. So I think children today are very lucky – but I *can't explain* this to my kids because they're too busy watching football on our 3D TV!

HELP WITH GRAMMAR
can/can't; could/couldn't

4 **a** Look at the phrases in blue in the article. Complete the rules with *can* and *could*.

● We use _____ + infinitive to say that something is possible in the present.

● We use _____ + infinitive to say that something was possible in the past.

b Look at the phrases in pink in the article. What is the negative of *can*? What is the negative of *could*?

c Fill in the gaps in these questions and short answers with *can, can't, could* or *couldn't*.

1 A ___*Can*___ you watch TV online?

   B Yes, you _____ ./No, you _____ .

2 A _____ you record programmes in 1974?

   B Yes, you _____ ./No, you _____ .

TIP ● *Can/can't* and *could/couldn't* are the same for all subjects (*I, you, he, she, it, we, they*).

d Check in GRAMMAR 6.3 ▶ p141.

HELP WITH LISTENING *can* and *can't*

5 **a** CD2 20 Listen to these sentences. Notice how we say *can* and *can't*. When is *can* stressed?

You can /kən/ watch TV programmes online.
I can't /ka:nt/ explain how lucky they are.
Can /kən/ you watch TV online?
Yes, you can /kæn/. No, you can't /ka:nt/.

b CD2 21 Listen to these sentences. Do you hear *can* or *can't*?

1 can't

---

6 CD2 22 PRONUNCIATION Listen and practise. Copy the stress and weak form of *can*.

You can /kən/ watch TV programmes online.

7 **a** Read about mobile phones. Fill in the gaps with *can, can't, could* or *couldn't*.

Motorola launched the first mobile phone in 1983, but you ¹ _could_ (+) only use it in a car because it needed a big battery. A few years later you ² _____ (+) buy a mobile that you ³ _____ (+) take to work – but it was in a suitcase!

In the early nineties you ⁴ _____ (+) buy a small mobile for $200, but you ⁵ _____ (–) send texts until 1995. The BlackBerry, launched in 1999, was one of the first phones you ⁶ _____ (+) use to go online. And you ⁷ _____ (–) buy a mobile with a camera in Europe until 2002.

These days most people ⁸ _____ (–) leave home without their mobile. You ⁹ _____ (+) use your phone to go online, make video calls and find your way with GPS. You ¹⁰ _____ (+) also download apps, watch TV programmes or play games. But a lot of people still ¹¹ _____ (–) remember to charge their phone or turn it off in the cinema!

b CD2 23 Listen and check your answers.

8 **a** Write four sentences with *could* and *couldn't* about your first mobile.

I could send texts with my first mobile.
I couldn't make video calls.

b Work in pairs. Compare sentences. Are any the same?

Get ready ... Get it right!

9 Make notes on what you can and can't do with these things.

● your mobile (and apps)   ● your computer/laptop   ● your TV

my mobile – I can make video calls, send texts, find restaurants ...

10 **a** Work in pairs. Ask questions to find out what you can do with the things in **9**, but your partner can't do.

Can you make video calls on your mobile?   Yes, I can.

b Tell the class two things you found out about your partner's mobile, computer or TV.

QUICK REVIEW Past time phrases Work in pairs. Take turns to ask your partner when he/she last did these things: cook a meal, eat out, play tennis, go clubbing, read a good book, go to the cinema. Ask follow-up questions. **A** *When did you last cook a meal?* **B** *Two weeks ago.* **A** *What did you cook?*

The one o'clock news

1 Work in groups. Discuss these questions.

1 Where do you usually get your news – the internet, the TV, the radio or newspapers?

2 Do you watch or listen to the news every day? If so, at what time of day?

3 What's in the news at the moment?

2 **a** Work in pairs. Which of these verbs do you know? What are the Past Simple forms of the irregular verbs? Check in VOCABULARY 6.4 ▶ p140.

REGULAR VERBS		IRREGULAR VERBS	
damage	sail	buy	lose
die	receive	find	put
crash	save	say	tell

b CD2 ▶24 PRONUNCIATION Listen and practise all the verbs in **2a** and their Past Simple forms.

3 **a** Before you listen, check these words/phrases with your teacher.

a train	a hospital	a storm	a couple
missing at sea		the coast	a helicopter
a boat	an envelope		

b Work in pairs. Look at photos A–D of some news stories. Which words are in each story, do you think?

4 **a** CD2 ▶25 Listen to the news and put photos A–D in order.

b Listen again and choose the correct answers.

1 **a** Over *16/60* people are in hospital after a train crash.

  b The train crashed in *London/Scotland*.

2 **a** There were storms in *Florida/California* last night.

  b *53/153* people died in the storms.

3 **a** Bill and Nancy Potter are *70/80* years old.

  b They are now *in Australia/missing at sea*.

4 **a** Joe Hall won over *£3/£13* million last night.

  b *Joe/His dog* chose the lottery numbers.

HELP WITH LISTENING Sentence stress (3)

5 **a** CD2 ▶25 Listen again to the first two sentences from the news. Notice the stressed words.

It's one o'clock and here's George Lucan with the news.

Over sixty people are in hospital after a train crash in Scotland this morning.

b Look at Audio Script CD2 ▶25 p160. Listen again and follow the stressed words.

Read all about it!

6 Look at the headlines on page 53 of two news reports from the next day. Which TV news stories are they about?

NewsWorld

`www.newsworld.com/couplefoundatsea`

COUPLE FOUND AT SEA

Bill and Nancy Potter, the 80-year-old British couple who were missing at sea, are now safe. A helicopter found them a hundred miles from the Australian coast and took them to a hospital in Sydney.

"The weather was beautiful when we left New Zealand," said Nancy. "But when we were about a hundred and fifty miles from Sydney there was a terrible storm. There was a lot of damage to the boat. Things were really bad and we couldn't use the radio because that was damaged too. All we could do was wait for help. We were very happy to see the helicopter. Those people saved our lives."

The couple bought the boat two years ago. "We wanted to be the first 80-year-old couple to sail round the world," said Bill. "Nancy wants to try again next year, but I'm not so sure."

1

DOG WINS LOTTERY!

Wednesday night's lottery winner Joe Hall received a cheque for over £13 million yesterday at the supermarket where he works. His dog, Max, who chose the winning numbers, was there with him.

"I usually choose the numbers," said 28-year-old Joe. "But I never win anything. So this time I asked Max to choose the numbers for me – and I won over £13 million!"

But how did the dog choose the numbers? "I wrote the numbers 1 to 50 on envelopes and put a dog biscuit in each envelope," Joe explained. "I put the envelopes in different places in my house and told Max to find the biscuits. Then I wrote down the numbers from the first six envelopes he found – and now I'm a millionaire!"

Now Joe wants Max to find him a girlfriend!

2

---

7 **a** Work in two groups. Group A, read report 1 and answer questions 1–5. Group B, read report 2 and answer questions a–e.

1 Where did the helicopter find Bill and Nancy?

2 Which city are they in now?

3 Where were they when the storm started?

4 Why didn't they use their radio?

5 When did they buy their boat?

a What did Joe do yesterday?

b What did he write on the envelopes?

c Where did he put them?

d Why did the dog want to find the envelopes?

e What does Joe want his dog to do now?

b Work in pairs. Student A, ask your partner questions a–e. Student B, ask your partner questions 1–5.

What happened?

8 **a** VIDEO▶6 CD2▶26 Watch or listen to four conversations about the news. Which news story is each conversation about?

b Watch or listen again. Match sentences 1–6 to responses a–f.

1 Over thirteen million pounds.   a Oh no, that's terrible.

2 His dog chose the numbers for him!   b Really?

3 Over sixty people are in hospital.   c You're joking!

4 Did you hear about the storms in Florida?   d Oh, dear. Are they OK?

5 Their boat was damaged in a storm.   e Oh, that's good.

6 Yes, a helicopter found them yesterday.   f Yes, isn't it awful?

REAL WORLD Talking about the news

9 **a** Fill in the gaps in the questions and responses with these words.

| was | happened | about | hear |

1 **A** Did you _____ about that train crash?

  B No, where _____ it?

2 **A** Did you read _____ the eighty-year-old couple and their boat?

  B No, what _____ ?

b Write responses a–f in 8b in the table.

good news	bad news	surprising news
		Really?

c Check in REAL WORLD 6.1 ▶ p141.

10 CD2▶27 PRONUNCIATION Listen and practise the questions and responses in **9a** and **9b**. Copy the stress and intonation.

Did you hear about that train crash?

No, where was it?

11 Work in pairs. Student A p106. Student B p111.

QUICK REVIEW Irregular verbs **Work in pairs. What can you remember about the four news stories from 6C? Compare ideas with another pair. Then check on p52 and p53.**

1 Work in groups. Discuss these questions.

1 Do you play video games? If so, discuss questions a–d. If not, discuss questions e–h.

   a What games do you play?
   b How often do you play?
   c When and where do you play?
   d What's your favourite game?
   e Why don't you play video games?
   f Do your friends or family play them?
   g Did you play when you were young?
   h Do you know any video games?

2 Do you think video games are a good or a bad thing? Why?/Why not?

2 a Before you read, check these words with your teacher.

a designer	art
an award	a hero
a villain	a princess
a prince	

b Read about Shigeru Miyamoto. Answer the questions.

1 What's Shigeru's job?
2 Who does he work for?
3 Where was he born?
4 Where did he study?
5 Is he married?
6 What was his wife's job at Nintendo?
7 Does he play a lot of video games?
8 Who is his favourite video game character?

3 CD2 ▶28 Listen to the beginning of a radio programme about Shigeru Miyamoto. Fill in gaps 1–7 in the fact file.

Shigeru Miyamoto
FACT FILE

Occupation
World-famous video game designer. Works for Nintendo. People call him the father of video games.

Born
Kyoto, Japan, November 16th [1]_____ .

Education
Studied art at Kanazawa College of Art from 1970 to [2]_____ .

Awards
Between 1998 and 2010 he won awards in the USA, the UK, [3]_____ and Spain.

Family life
Married with two children, a boy and a girl. Met his wife, Yasuko, when she was a manager at Nintendo in Japan.

Interesting facts
Doesn't play video games very often. Usually goes to work by [4]_____ . Can write with both hands, but usually uses his left hand. Can play the guitar and write [5]_____ .

Once said
"They say video games are [6]_____ for you. But that's what they said about rock 'n' roll."

The video games
Shigeru designed the first Mario Brothers game in [7]_____ and Mario is his favourite video game character.

All Mario Bros. video games have **a story**. **The story** always has **a hero**, **a princess** and **a villain**. **The villain** wants to marry **the princess**, so he takes her to **a place** where **the hero** can't find her. But **the hero** always finds **the place** and saves **the princess** from **the villain**. And that's **the end** of the game.

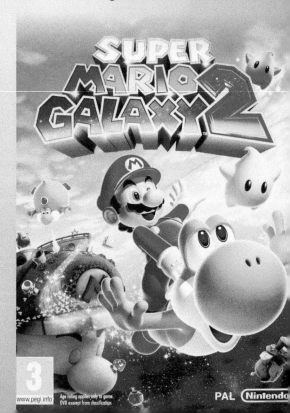

PAL Nintendo

HELP WITH VOCABULARY
Articles: *a*, *an* and *the*

4 **a** Look at the words in bold in these sentences. Then complete the rules with *a* or *the*.

*People call him **the father** of video games.*

*The story always has **a hero**, **a princess** and **a villain**.*

***The villain** wants to marry **the princess**.*

1 We use _____ when we know which thing, person, place, etc. because there is only one.

2 We use _____ or *an* to talk about things or people for the first time.

3 We use _____ to talk about a person or a thing for the second, third, fourth, etc. time.

TIP • We use *the* in some fixed phrases: *at **the** weekend, in **the** evening, go to **the** cinema,* etc.

b Check in VOCABULARY 6.5 p140.

5 Work in pairs. Look at the words in bold in the last paragraph of the fact file. Match the words in bold to rules 1–3 in **4a**.

6 **a** Read about a new video game. Fill in the gaps with *a*, *an* and *the*.

I bought ¹ a new video game at ² _____ weekend.
³ _____ game is about ⁴ _____ beautiful princess.
One day ⁵ _____ princess goes for ⁶ _____ walk. She meets
⁷ _____ old man and ⁸ _____ beautiful white dog. ⁹ _____
old man takes ¹⁰ _____ princess away because he wants to
marry her. But ¹¹ _____ dog saves ¹² _____ princess from
¹³ _____ old man. Then at ¹⁴ _____ end of ¹⁵ _____ game,
you find out that ¹⁶ _____ dog is really ¹⁷ _____ prince.

b Work in pairs. Compare answers.

7 **a** Choose the correct word.

1 Did you have *a/the* big lunch yesterday?

2 Is there *a/the* park near your home?

3 Did you go to *a/the* capital city of another country last year?

4 Do you often go to *a/the* cinema at *a/the* weekend?

5 What was *a/the* last film you saw?

6 Is there *a/the* TV programme you watch every week?

b Work in pairs. Ask and answer the questions. Ask follow-up questions if possible.

HELP WITH PRONUNCIATION
Past Simple of regular verbs

1 **a** 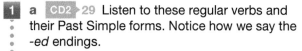 **CD2 29** Listen to these regular verbs and their Past Simple forms. Notice how we say the *-ed* endings.

1 watch → watch**ed** /t/   ask → ask**ed** /t/

2 stay → stay**ed** /d/   enjoy → enjoy**ed** /d/

3 start → start**ed** /ɪd/   want → want**ed** /ɪd/

TIP • When a regular verb ends in /t/ or /d/, *-ed* is pronounced /ɪd/.

b Listen again and practise.

2 **a** Work in pairs. Which Past Simple form has an /ɪd/ ending?

1 moved   loved   ⟨wanted⟩

2 downloaded   liked   played

3 lived   crashed   chatted

4 listened   hated   worked

5 recorded   travelled   finished

6 walked   visited   phoned

b **CD2 30** Listen and check. Listen again and practise.

3 Work in pairs. Take turns to say a verb from **1a** or **2a**. Your partner says the Past Simple form.

continue2learn

■ Vocabulary, Grammar and Real World

■ **Extra Practice 6 and Progress Portfolio 6** p120

■ **Language Summary 6** p140

■ **6A–D** Workbook p30

■ **Self-study DVD-ROM 6** with Review Video

■ Reading and Writing

■ **Portfolio 6** Text me! Workbook p74
Reading entertainment adjectives
Writing messages (2); a text message

Pair and Group Work: Student/Group A

1A 11 p9

a Work with your partner. Ask questions about cards A, B and C. Write the names and countries. Don't look at your partner's cards.

Card A. What's her name?

How do you spell that?

Where's she from?

A

NAME _____

COUNTRY

B

NAME _____

COUNTRY

C

NAME _____

COUNTRY

D

NAME Zhou Jingwei

COUNTRY China

E

NAME Luciana Riquelme

COUNTRY Argentina

F

NAME Mikhail Vasilyev

COUNTRY Russia

b Answer your partner's questions about cards D, E and F.

c Check your answers and spelling with your partner.

2A 13 p17

a Work on your own. Guess the things your partner has got, but don't talk to him/her. Put a tick (✓) or a cross (✗) in the *your guess* column.

	your guess	your partner's answer

b Look at the pictures. Write questions with *you*.

Have you got a mobile?

c Work with your partner. Ask and answer your questions. Put a tick or a cross in the *your partner's answer* column. Are your guesses correct?

d Work with a new partner. Tell him/her five things your first partner has/hasn't got.

1B 12 p11

a Work on your own. Look at the hotel conference list. Write *yes/no* questions to check the information in pink on the list (Mr = 🔺 Mrs = 🔺).

Is Mrs Ramos a teacher?

b Work with your partner. Take turns to ask your questions from **a**. Tick (✓) the correct information. Change the wrong information.

> Is Mrs Ramos a teacher?

> No, she isn't. She's a doctor.

c Compare answers with another student A.

Mrs Ramos isn't a teacher. She's a doctor.

Conference Guest List

name	job	nationality	room
Mrs Ramos	a teacher	Mexican	216
Mr Demir	a manager	Turkish	112
Mr Wong	an actor	Japanese	204
Mrs Ivanova	a teacher	Russian	307
Mr Fisher	a mechanic		
Mrs Fisher	a lawyer	Australian	209
Mr Bruni	a builder	Italian	108
Mrs Bruni	a musician		

2C 13 p21

a You are a customer. Choose one of these films. Buy two tickets from your partner. Fill in the times and the prices for your film. You start.

48 Hours	Time: _____ £ _____
Three Long Years	Time: _____ £ _____
Two Weeks on Sunday	Time: _____ £ _____

b You are a ticket seller. Look at the times and prices of the films at your cinema. Sell tickets to your partner. Your partner starts.

Today's films

60 Seconds	7.10
Nine Months	8.25
A Day in the Life	9.35

| Adults £10.50 | Children £8 |

c Do **a** and **b** again. Buy tickets for different films. Change the number and type of tickets you buy.

3B 10 p27

a Work on your own. Choose the correct words in phrases 1–5.

	name	name
1 watch TV *every/in* evening		
2 do sport *in/on* Saturdays		
3 go to bed after midnight *in/at* the week		
4 go to concerts *in/at* the weekends		
5 eat out *at/every* week		

b Make questions with *you* with phrases 1–5 in **a**.

1 Do you watch TV every evening?

c Ask other students in the class your questions. Try to find two people who answer *yes* for each question. Write their names in the table.

d Tell the class about the people in your table.

Kristina and Michiko watch TV every evening.

4B 9 p35

Jo is 29 and she's a lawyer. In her free time she watches TV, goes shopping and reads a lot. On Saturday evenings she usually goes to the cinema or eats out – she loves Chinese food. She doesn't like sport and she hates football. Her favourite music is rock and she also likes jazz. She likes animals but hasn't got any pets.

4B 10 c p35

MARK   I like Kim very much and we like a lot of the same things. We both go to the cinema a lot and we both really like animals. But she doesn't like the same music as me and she hasn't got a TV – I don't believe that! Yes, I'd like to see her again. She's very beautiful.

KIM   Sorry, I don't like Mark very much. He talks about football and TV programmes all the time and I don't like watching TV. Also, we don't like the same music – and music's very important to me. I don't want a second date with him. Sorry.

5A **11** p41

a Work on your own. Write questions with *you* or *your* about when you were thirteen.

	you	your partner
1 / happy at school? *Were you happy at school?*		
2 Who / best friend?		
3 / good at languages?		
4 What / favourite food?		
5 What / favourite TV programme?		

b Write your answers in the *you* column.

c Work with your partner. Ask and answer your questions. Write your partner's answers in the table.

d Tell another student about you and your partner when you were thirteen.

I was happy at school when I was thirteen, but Paola wasn't.

6C **11** p53

a Work on your own. Read about the news stories. Check you understand all the words.

Big storm
Mexico
13 people died

**Man who found
1 million dollars**
under the kitchen floor
gave money to a hospital

**Tourists missing
in Africa**
Sahara desert
lost for 2 weeks
other tourists found them –
they're OK now

**Man
tries to
post ma**

A woman who
tioned about t'
on Monday m
in the sleepy v
witness said th
man was in his

b Work with your partner. Take turns to tell each other about the news stories. Use these phrases.

Did you hear/read about … ?   No, what happened?
No, where was it?   Oh, that's good.   Oh no, that's terrible.
Oh, dear. Are they OK?   You're joking!   Really?

Pair and Group Work: Student/Group B

1A 11 p9

a Work with your partner. Answer his/her questions about cards A, B and C.

A

NAME **Natalia Grabowska**

COUNTRY
Poland

B

NAME **Eduardo Acosta**

COUNTRY
Mexico

C

NAME **Felicity Wheaton**

COUNTRY
the UK

D

NAME

COUNTRY

E

NAME

COUNTRY

F

NAME

COUNTRY

b Ask questions about cards D, E and F. Write the names and countries. Don't look at your partner's cards.

Card D. What's his name?

How do you spell that?

Where's he from?

c Check your answers and spelling with your partner.

2A 13 p17

a Work on your own. Guess the things your partner has got, but don't talk to him/her. Put a tick (✓) or a cross (✗) in the *your guess* column.

	your guess	your partner's answer

b Look at the pictures. Write questions with *you*.

Have you got a computer?

c Work with your partner. Ask and answer your questions. Put a tick or a cross in the *your partner's answer* column. Are your guesses correct?

d Work with a new partner. Tell him/her five things your first partner has/hasn't got.

1B 12 p11

a Work on your own. Look at the hotel conference list. Write *yes/no* questions to check the information in pink on the list (Mr = 🔼 Mrs = 🔼).

Is Mr Demir a waiter?

b Work with your partner. Take turns to ask your questions from **a**. Tick (✓) the correct information. Change the wrong information.

> Is Mr Demir a waiter?

> No, he isn't. He's a manager.

c Compare answers with another student B.

Mr Demir isn't a waiter. He's a manager.

Conference Guest List

name	job	nationality	room
Mrs Ramos	a doctor	Spanish	216
Mr Demir	a waiter	Turkish	112
Mr Wong	a police officer	American	204
Mrs Ivanova	a waitress	Russian	317
Mr Fisher	a mechanic	British	209
Mrs Fisher	an accountant	British	209
Mr Bruni	a builder		
		Italian	106
Mrs Bruni	an actress		

2C 13 p21

a You are a ticket seller. Look at the times and prices of the films at your cinema. Sell tickets to your partner. Your partner starts.

Today's **films**

48 Hours	**7.20**
Three Long Years	**8.45**
Two Weeks on Sunday	**9.10**
Adults £9.95	**Children** £7.35

b You are a customer. Choose one of these films. Buy two tickets from your partner. Fill in the times and the prices for your film. You start.

60 Seconds	Time: _____ £ _____
Nine Months	Time: _____ £ _____
A Day in the Life	Time: _____ £ _____

c Do **a** and **b** again. Buy tickets for different films. Change the number and type of tickets you buy.

3B 10 p27

a Work on your own. Choose the correct words in phrases 1–5.

	name	name
1 watch TV *in/on* the morning		
2 go shopping *every/in* Saturday		
3 go for a drink *at/on* Friday evenings		
4 go to the cinema *at/ every* month		
5 work *at/in* the weekends		

b Make questions with *you* with phrases 1–5 in **a**.

1 Do you watch TV in the morning?

c Ask other students in the class your questions. Try to find two people who answer *yes* for each question. Write their names in the table.

d Tell the class about the people in your table.

Gabriela and Rudi watch TV in the morning.

4B 9 p35

Susie's 23 and she's a waitress. She really loves dance music but she doesn't like rock music. She doesn't go to restaurants very often but she loves fast food. On Saturday evenings she goes clubbing with friends or stays in and watches TV. She doesn't like watching sport on TV but she goes swimming a lot. And she has seven cats!

4B 10 c p35

MARK   Jo and I like some of the same things. We both like going to the cinema and eating Chinese food. But she talks about books and shopping *all* the time. We both like rock music, but she hates sport and I love it! No, I don't want to see her again. Sorry!

JO   I *really* like Mark. He's very different from me, but that's a good thing, I think. I hate football, but he loves it. And he plays video games all the time and he never reads books. But yes, I'd like a second date with him. Definitely. He's very nice.

5A **11** p41

a Work on your own. Write questions with *you* or *your* about when you were thirteen.

	you	your partner
1 / tall for your age? *Were you tall for your age?*		
2 Who / favourite teacher?		
3 / good at sport?		
4 Who / favourite singer?		
5 Where / thirteenth birthday party?		

b Write your answers in the *you* column.

c Work with your partner. Ask and answer your questions. Write your partner's answers in the table.

d Tell another student about you and your partner when you were thirteen.

I was tall for my age when I was thirteen, but Johann wasn't.

6C **11** p53

a Work on your own. Read about the news stories. Check you understand all the words.

3 students lost in Brazil
Amazon jungle
lost for six days
helicopter found them
they're OK now

Plane crash
in Africa
over 80 people died

Man who won the lottery
dog ate ticket
gave dog to friend

Planes at airp
why the

Tuesday morn:
a number of k
and have made
to the press at
"I see no reaso
said Mr Dawk

b Work with your partner. Take turns to tell each other about the news stories. Use these phrases.

Did you hear/read about … ?   No, what happened?
No, where was it?   Oh, that's good.   Oh no, that's terrible.
Oh, dear. Are they OK?   You're joking!   Really?

Pair and Group Work: Other exercises

4B 10 c p35

MARK Susie's very nice. We both like the same things – watching TV and doing sport. Also, she has lots of cats and I really like cats. She doesn't like rock music very much, but that's OK. Yes, I'd like a second date with her. Yes, please!

SUSIE Mark? Yes, I like him. We both do a lot of sport. I like swimming and he likes football. And we both watch a lot of TV and DVDs, so that's a good thing. Do I want to see him again? Yes, why not? Maybe we can go clubbing next time.

3D 2 b p30

Are you an early bird or a night owl?

1	a 1 point	b 2 points	c 3 points
2	a 2 points	b 1 point	c 3 points
3	a 3 points	b 1 point	c 2 points
4	a 3 points	b 2 points	c 1 point
5	a 2 points	b 1 point	c 3 points
6	a 1 point	b 2 points	c 3 points

6–9 points:
You're definitely an early bird. You probably get up very early and do lots of things before lunchtime. But you're probably not a good person to go to an all-night party with!

10–13 points:
You're not a night owl or an early bird – so you're probably an afternoon person! You probably get up early in the week and then sleep a lot at the weekend.

14–18 points:
You're definitely an night owl. You probably go out a lot in the evening and watch TV late at night. But you're probably not a good person to have breakfast with!

5B 11 p43

a Work on your own. Choose five to eight of these events in your life. Write the year/month when these things happened on a timeline.

- born
- brother/sister born
- start/leave school
- move to a new school
- start learning English
- go to your first concert/football match
- start/leave university
- meet your first girlfriend/boyfriend
- move to a different town/city
- meet your husband/wife
- start your first job/a new job
- get married
- have a child
- meet your best friend

b Work with your partner. Take turns to tell each other about your timeline. Ask questions to get more information.

c Tell another student three things about your partner's life.

BORN IN ...   NOW

Extra Practice 1

Language Summary 1 p128

1A p8

1 **a** Find twelve countries (→↓).

```
R  E  B  R  A  Z  I  L  A  A
G  E  R  M  A  N  Y  R  R  R
U  P  S  E  D  F  P  U  G
K  I  T  A  L  Y  O  S  E
F  R  A  N  C  E  L  S  N
L  A  R  U  S  A  A  I  T
L  O  N  C  H  I  N  A  I
T  U  R  K  E  Y  D  W  N
A  U  S  T  R  A  L  I  A
```

b Write the nationalities.
Brazil → Brazilian

2 Fill in the gaps with *'m*, *'re*, *are* or *'s*.

A What¹ *'s* your name?
B My name² _____ Ali.
A Where ³_____ you from?
B I⁴ _____ from Egypt.

A Where ⁵_____ they from?
B They⁶ _____ from Australia.
A What ⁷_____ their names?
B His name⁸_____ Jason and her name⁹_____ Kylie.

A Hi, Jo. How ¹⁰_____ you?
B I¹¹_____ fine, thanks. And you?
A I¹²_____ OK, thanks.

3 Choose the correct words.

1 What's *you/your* name?
2 It's *she/her* dictionary.
3 *We/Our* 're Japanese.
4 *My/I* 'm from Turkey.
5 It's *he/his* computer.
6 *They're/Their* Spanish.
7 *You're/Your* in room C.
8 *It's/Its* an MP3 player.
9 What are *they/their* names?
10 *We/Our* names are Colin and Henry.
11 Where's *you/your* book?
12 *We/Our* 're students and Peter's *we/our* teacher.

1B p10

4 Fill in the gaps in these jobs with *a, e, i, o* or *u*. Then put *a* or *an* in the boxes.

1 [a] l a wy e r
2 [ ] d _ ct _ r
3 [ ] m _ s _ c _ _ n
4 [ ] w _ tr _ ss
5 [ ] _ cc _ _ nt _ nt
6 [ ] m _ n _ g _ r
7 [ ] _ ng _ n _ _ r
8 [ ] p _ l _ ce _ ff _ c _ r
9 [ ] m _ ch _ n _ c
10 [ ] cl _ _ n _ r
11 [ ] s _ l _ s _ ss _ st _ nt
12 [ ] t _ _ ch _ r

5 Make these sentences negative. Write correct sentences.

1 Julia Roberts is Polish.
Julia Roberts isn't Polish. She's American.

2 Leonardo DiCaprio is an accountant.
3 David and Victoria Beckham are from Spain.
4 Pepsi and Coca-Cola are British companies.
5 Sydney is in the USA.
6 Ferraris are German cars.
7 Liverpool and Manchester are in Australia.

6 **a** Fill in the gaps in these questions with *Am, Are* or *Is*.

1 _Are_ you a student?
2 _____ she an actress?
3 _____ they Argentinian?
4 _____ I in room 201?
5 _____ it an English hotel?
6 _____ he from Mexico?
7 _____ we in room B?
8 _____ you from London?

b Write positive and negative short answers for the questions in **6a**.

1 *Yes, I am. No, I'm not.*

1C p12

7 Write questions with *your* for these answers.

1 Jones. *What's your surname?*
2 It's Anna.
3 I'm British.
4 67, West Road, London.
5 SE13 7GR.
6 My mobile number's 07954 362313.
7 It's 020 7946 0840.
8 jane22@webmail.com.

1D p14

8 Write the plurals.

1 a camera *cameras*
2 a surname
3 a watch
4 a dictionary
5 a dress
6 a pencil
7 a tooth
8 a woman
9 a man
10 an address

Progress Portfolio 1

Tick the things you can do in English.

- [ ] I can introduce people.
- [ ] I can say countries and nationalities.
- [ ] I can say and understand the numbers 0–100.
- [ ] I can talk about jobs.
- [ ] I can ask for, give and understand personal information (name, etc.).
- [ ] I can ask people to repeat things.

What do you need to study again? See Self-study DVD-ROM 1.

Extra Practice 2

Language Summary 2 p130

2A p16

1 Write the adjectives. Then write their opposites.

1	ewn	*new*	o*ld*
2	epahc	c_____	e_____
3	lamls	s_____	b_____
4	swol	s_____	f_____
5	lygu	u_____	b_____
6	ysea	e_____	d_____
7	uogny	y_____	o_____
8	dogo	g_____	b_____
9	leayr	e_____	l_____
10	ghrit	r_____	w_____

2 Choose the correct words.

1 She*'ve*/*'s* got an old bike.
2 We *haven't/hasn't* got a car.
3 They*'ve*/*'s* got a new DVD player.
4 Jo *haven't/hasn't* got a camera.
5 I*'ve*/*'s* got a new laptop.
6 He *haven't/hasn't* got an MP3 player.
7 They *haven't/hasn't* got a very big car.
8 You*'ve*/*'s* got a nice watch.
9 She *haven't/hasn't* got a pen.
10 We*'ve*/*'s* got a beautiful cat.

3 Fill in the gaps with *have, has, haven't* or *hasn't*.

1 A ___*Have*___ you got a computer?
  B Yes, I have.
2 A _____ Mona got a laptop?
  B No, she _____ .
3 A _____ you got a dictionary?
  B Yes, I _____ .
4 A _____ they got a new DVD player?
  B No, they _____ .
5 A _____ he got a camera?
  B Yes, he _____ .
6 A _____ we got his address?
  B Yes, we _____ .
7 A _____ Bob got a car?
  B No, he _____ .
8 A _____ they got a big TV?
  B Yes, they _____ .

2B p18

4 Complete these sentences.

1 Your mother's son is …
  your brother
2 Your mother's daughter is …
3 Your son's children are …
4 Your mother's brother is …
5 Your father's sister is …
6 Your father's parents are …
7 Your mother's brother's daughter is …

5 Look at these sentences. Does *'s* mean *is*, *has* or possessive?

1 Jack**'s** got a camera. *'s = has*
2 She**'s** got an MP3 player.
3 Mark**'s** unemployed.
4 This is Ed**'s** baby.
5 She**'s** from Prague.
6 That**'s** Pam**'s** husband.

2C p20

6 **a** Put these times in order.

twenty to ten *1*	five to ten
quarter past ten	ten past ten
quarter to ten	ten to ten
twenty-five past ten	half past ten

b Write the times in **6a** in a different way.

twenty to ten → *nine forty*

7 Read this conversation at a cinema. Fill in the gaps with these words.

~~Can~~	Here	course	Thanks
film	tickets	That's	starts
time	much		

A ¹ *Can* I have two ² _____ for *24 Hours*, please?
B Yes, of ³ _____ .
A How ⁴ _____ is that?
B ⁵ _____ £18, please.
A ⁶ _____ you are. What ⁷ _____ is the film?
B It ⁸ _____ at six fifty.
A Right. ⁹ _____ a lot.
B You're welcome. Enjoy the ¹⁰ _____ .

2D p22

8 Look at pictures 1–6. Complete the words. Then fill in the gaps with these prepositions.

~~by~~	under	in	behind
in front of	on		

1 The plant's *by* the d *o o r*.
2 The plant's _____ the b ___ .
3 The plant's _____ the d ____ .
4 The plant's _____ the s ___ .
5 The plant's _____ the b _____ .
6 The plant's _____ the c _____ t _____ .

Extra Practice 3

Language Summary 3 p132

3A p24

1 Read about Vince's day. Fill in the gaps with these verbs.

> ~~live~~   work   finish   start
> go   leave   get
> get up   have (x2)

1 I _live_ **in Brighton**.
2 I _____ **at 7.00**.
3 I _____ home **at 8.30**.
4 I _____ work **at 9.00**.
5 I _____ **in a school**.
6 I _____ lunch **in a café**.
7 I _____ work **at 5.30**.
8 I _____ home **at 6.00**.
9 I _____ dinner **at home**.
10 I _____ to bed at **11.30**.

2 Complete these questions with *you* for the words/phrases in bold in **1**.

1 Where _do you live_ ?
2 What time _____ ?
3 When _____ ?
4 What time _____ ?
5 Where _____ ?
6 Where _____ ?
7 When _____ ?
8 What time _____ ?
9 Where _____ ?
10 When _____ ?

3B p26

3 Match a word/phrase in A to a word/phrase in B.

A	B
go	your family
visit	in
do	out
stay	sport
have	the cinema
go to	coffee with friends

go	concerts
watch	shopping
eat	friends
go to	a drink
phone	TV
go for	out

4

a Fill in the gaps with *in, on* or *at*.

1 I get up early _in_ the week.
2 They work _____ the weekend.
3 Gavin and Ruby eat out _____ Friday evenings.
4 My brother and I go to the cinema _____ Sundays.
5 Tom and Bob work _____ night.
6 I phone my mum and dad _____ the mornings.
7 My parents have lunch _____ one o'clock.
8 We do sport _____ the afternoon.
9 I phone my son _____ Saturdays.
10 I get up _____ half past six.

b Make the sentences in **4a** negative.

1 *I don't get up early in the week.*

3C p28

5 What do you say on these special days?

1 your sister's birthday
   Happy birthday!
2 a friend's wedding
3 1st January
4 the birth of a baby
5 a wedding anniversary

6 Complete the words in this conversation.

A What ¹s _hall_ we ²g_____ Maya for her birthday?
B What ³a_____ a new watch?
A No, I don't ⁴t_____ so. She's got a nice watch.
B Why ⁵d_____ we get her a radio?
A ⁶M_____ . But she's got an MP3 player.
B I know! ⁷L_____ get her a camera.
A Yes, ⁸t_____ a good ⁹i_____ . Where's your credit card?
B *My* credit card?!

3D p30

7 Make sentences with these words.

1 Sundays / work / I / usually / on .
   I usually work on Sundays.
2 I / in / never / the afternoon / sleep .
3 on / I / Saturday / at home / sometimes / 'm / evenings .
4 often / go out / friends / the week / in / I / with .
5 always / My / birthday / remember / friends / my .
6 New Year's Eve / on / hardly ever / are / at home / My parents .
7 tired / evenings / usually / 'm / on / very / Friday / I .

8 Choose the correct words.

1 Do you know *he*/(*him*)?
2 Is *she/her* a doctor?
3 They email *we/us* a lot.
4 How do you know *she/her*?
5 I don't understand *they/them*.
6 Why don't *they/them* phone *I/me*?

Progress Portfolio 3

Tick the things you can do in English.

☐ I can describe my daily routine.
☐ I can talk about my free time activities and say when I do them.
☐ I can ask people about their routines and free time.
☐ I can use phrases for special days.
☐ I can ask for, make and respond to suggestions.
☐ I can say how often I do things.

> What do you need to study again? See Self-study DVD-ROM 3.

Extra Practice 4

Language Summary 4 p135

4A p32

1 Match the verbs to the words/phrases.

go	to music
go	running
listen	photos
take	swimming
go	tennis
play	to the radio
read	clubbing
listen	books or magazines
go	video games
play	sport on TV
go to	cycling
watch	the gym

2 **a** Add *-s*, *-es* or – to the verbs in these sentences.

1 My son watch *es* TV a lot.
2 Barry take__ good photos.
3 Paula go__ out on Saturdays.
4 Ian and Liz work__ at home.
5 My sister live__ in the USA.
6 Our class finish__ at 8.30.
7 Luke's parents like__ jazz.
8 Rob watch__ sport on TV.
9 We go__ out on Fridays.
10 She do__ a lot of sport.

b Make the sentences negative.

1 *My son doesn't watch TV a lot.*

4B p34

3 Look at the pictures. Fill in the gaps with the correct form of these words/phrases.

~~love~~ hate really like don't like is/are OK quite like like

1  He *loves* cats.
2  We ________ cooking.
3  She ________ dogs.
4  I ________ jazz.
5  I think tennis ________ .
6  They ________ football.
7  He ________ shopping for clothes.

4 **a** Make questions with these words.

1 What / do / does / he ?
What does he do?
2 work / does / Where / he ?
3 like / rock music / he / Does ?
4 What / she / on Friday nights / does / do ?
5 What / like / she / does / food ?
6 she / watch / Does / on TV / sport ?

b Fill in the gaps with the correct form of the verb in brackets and complete the short answers. Then match answers a–f to questions 1–6.

a He *teaches* English. (teach) *1*
b She ______ clubbing. (go)
c She ______ Italian food. (like)
d He ______ in Spain. (work)
e Yes, she ______ . She ______ football and tennis. (love)
f No, he ______ . He ______ dance music and jazz. (like)

4C p36

5 Betty is in a restaurant. Fill in the gaps with these phrases.

~~to order~~ can I have I'd like Would you like (x3) the bill to drink a glass of that's all

WAITER Would you like [1] *to order* now?
BETTY Yes, [2] ________ the burger and chips, please.
W What would you like [3] ________ ?
B I'd like [4] ________ red wine, please.
W [5] ________ anything else?
B No, [6] ________ , thanks.
W [7] ________ a dessert?
B Yes, [8] ________ the apple pie, please?
W [9] ________ tea or coffee?
B No, thanks. Can I have [10] ________ , please?
W Certainly, madam.

4D p38

6 **a** Find fifteen words for food and drink. (→↓).

C	H	E	E	S	E	F	O	T
B	Y	T	O	A	S	T	F	O
A	E	F	R	U	I	T	I	M
N	E	G	G	S	L	K	S	A
A	B	R	E	A	D	E	H	T
N	T	E	A	G	M	X	A	O
A	P	P	L	E	R	I	C	E
M	E	A	T	S	L	L	W	S
M	I	L	K	O	K	J	A	M

b Which words are countable (C)? Which are uncountable (U)?

cheese U *banana C*

7 Fill in the gaps with *a*, *an* or –.

1 Do you have – sugar?
2 Can I have ______ croissant?
3 I don't like ______ olives.
4 Would you like ______ biscuit?
5 I love ______ chicken soup.
6 I always have ______ egg sandwich for lunch.

Progress Portfolio 4

Tick the things you can do in English.

- ☐ I can talk about other people's routines and free time activities.
- ☐ I can say what I like and don't like.
- ☐ I can ask and answer questions about people I don't know.
- ☐ I can say and understand words for food and drink.
- ☐ I can order something to eat and drink in a restaurant.
- ☐ I can offer things to people.
- ☐ I can ask people for things.

What do you need to study again? See Self-study DVD-ROM 4.

Extra Practice 5

Language Summary 5 p138

5A p40

1 Write the opposites of these adjectives.

1 ill *well*
2 happy
3 hot
4 lucky
5 different
6 tall
7 friendly
8 boring
9 fantastic
10 quiet

2 Choose the correct words.

1 I (was)/were at home yesterday.
2 Jack and I *was/were* in Rome last week.
3 The film *was/were* amazing!
4 My uncle *was/were* a doctor.
5 I *wasn't/weren't* here last year.
6 He *wasn't/weren't* very well.
7 You *wasn't/weren't* here on Monday.
8 They *wasn't/weren't* born in the UK.

3 Make questions with these words.

1 were / night / you / Where / last ?
   Where were you last night?
2 they / at home / yesterday / Were / afternoon ?
3 the party / Was / son / your / at ?
4 at / were / 5 p.m. / you / Where ?
5 born / were / Where / you ?
6 they / When / born / were ?
7 in / he / Was / born / London ?

5B p42

4 a Choose the correct verbs.

1 (have)/write children
2 win/make a film
3 meet/study English
4 leave/meet school
5 make/become famous
6 become/write a book
7 win/meet a lot of money
8 move/leave house

b Write the Past Simple of the correct verbs in **4a**.

have → had

5 a Read about Beryl, Jason's grandmother. Fill in gaps 1–8 with the Past Simple of these verbs.

be	meet (x2)	have
go	live	move	get

I [1] *was* born [a]in 1954 and my family [2]_____ [b]in Liverpool. In 1973 I [3]_____ my husband, Albert, at [c]a party and we [4]_____ married [d]on May 1st 1975.
We [5]_____ our first child, Matt, [e]in 1977. Matt [6]_____ to [f]Spain on holiday in 1997 and [7]_____ [g]his wife there. They [8]_____ to Bristol [h]in 1999 and they have four children now.

b Make questions for the words/phrases a–h in bold.

a *When was Beryl born?*
b *Where did her family live?*

5C p44

6 Match the verbs to the phrases.

go	for the weekend
write	to a party
clean	an email
go away	the car
do	for a walk
have	with friends
stay	a great time
go	the washing

7 Choose the correct response in these conversations.

1 A I won £50,000 yesterday.
  B *Oh, nice./Wow!*
2 A Tim and I went to Venice last week.
  B *What a shame./Really?*
3 A I was ill last weekend.
  B *Oh, dear./Oh, nice.*
4 A I met the President of the USA last month.
  B *You're joking!/Oh, dear.*
5 A I stayed in all weekend.
  B *Oh, right./What a shame.*
6 A I went clubbing last night.
  B *Oh, dear./Oh, nice.*

5D p46

8 a Write the missing letters in these adjectives.

1 c *r* ow *d* ed
2 d _ rt _
3 ex _ _ t _ d
4 p _ _ r
5 dan _ er _ us
6 cl _ _ n
7 e _ pt _
8 r _ c _
9 b _ r _ d
10 s _ f _

b Match the opposite adjectives in **8a**.

crowded, empty

9 Choose the correct words.

1 Sorry, I can't come today. I'm (too)/quite busy.
2 Let's go to that restaurant. It's *too/really* nice.
3 He's a *very/too* important man.
4 Mike is always *quite/too* lucky.
5 Kim's husband is *too/quite* rich.
6 That film was *too/quite* long. I went to sleep after 5 hours!
7 This book is *really/too* interesting.

Progress Portfolio 5

Tick the things you can do in English.

☐ I can describe people and places.
☐ I can talk about things that happened in my life.
☐ I can ask questions about things other people did in the past.
☐ I can say and understand years.
☐ I can talk about what I did last weekend.
☐ I can respond to people's news and ask follow-up questions.

What do you need to study again? See Self-study DVD-ROM 5.

119

Extra Practice 6

6A p48

1 Fill in the gaps with these words.

> ~~website~~   get   blog   emails
> online   download   chat
> WiFi   use   search engine

1 I don't have a favourite _website_ .
2 Paul sends lots of _____
   every day.
3 Did you _____ my email?
4 This café has _____ .
5 I _____ the internet for my
   food shopping.
6 Do you always use the same
   _____ ?
7 My kids _____ a lot of videos
   and music.
8 I _____ to my sister online
   every day.
9 I often go _____ and read
   my friend's _____ .

2 Fill in the gaps with *didn't*, *wasn't*
or *weren't*.

1 I _didn't_ go to bed late last night.
2 I _____ watch TV yesterday.
3 My parents _____ go to
   university.
4 I _____ at home last week.
5 My parents _____ born in
   the UK.
6 I _____ like my first school.
7 I _____ have a holiday last year.
8 I _____ late for work last week.

3 Fill in the gaps with the Past
Simple of the verbs in brackets,
did or *didn't*.

A ¹ _Did_ you _go out_ yesterday
   evening? (go out)
B Yes, I ² _____ . I ³ _____ to see
   my sister. (go)
A What ⁴ _____ you _____ ? (do)
B We ⁵ _____ a DVD. (watch)
A ⁶ _____ you _____ it? (enjoy)
B No, I ⁷ _____ . It ⁸ _____
   terrible! (be)
A ⁹ _____ you _____ at your
   sister's? (stay)
B No I ¹⁰ _____ . I ¹¹ _____
   home. (come)

6B p50

4 Choose the correct words.

1 I didn't *send*/*get* your text. Can
   you *send*/*get* it again?
2 Remember to *turn on*/*turn off*
   your phone before the film starts.
3 What was the last *app*/*GPS*
   you downloaded?
4 Which *programme*/*channel* is
   the football on?
5 I need a new *charge*/*battery* for
   my mobile.
6 Do you *charge*/*record* your
   phone every night?
7 Can you *turn on*/*turn off* the
   TV? My favourite *programme*/
   channel is on now.

5 Make sentences with these
words.

1 ago / I / two / him / days / met .
   I met him two days ago.
2 born / He / eighteenth / the / in /
   century / was .
3 night / out / I / last / went .
4 days / arrived / She / ago / ten .
5 2011 / to Paris / My parents /
   in / went .
6 in / famous / was / the eighties /
   His father .

6 Choose the correct words.

1 Excuse me. *Can*/*Could* you
   make video calls on this mobile?
2 You *can't*/*couldn't* go online
   in 1970.
3 You *can*/*could* buy mobiles in
   the 1990s.
4 Sorry, we *can't*/*couldn't* come
   to your party next week.
5 Look! You *can*/*could* see my
   house from here.
6 He *can't*/*couldn't* go to work
   last week.
7 *Can*/*Could* you watch TV on
   your new mobile?
8 Two years ago you *can't*/
   couldn't buy these phones.
9 You *can*/*could* use Google
   in 1998.
10 Help! I *can't*/*couldn't* swim!

6C p52

7 Fill in the gaps with these words.

> ~~hear~~   read   where   joking
> died   what   Really   terrible

A Did you ¹ _hear_ about that
   plane crash?
B No, ² _____ was it?
A In the USA. 310 people ³ _____ .
B Oh no, that's ⁴ _____ .
A Did you ⁵ _____ about the
   woman who won the lottery?
B No, ⁶ _____ happened?
A Her baby chose the numbers.
B ⁷ _____ ? You're ⁸ _____ !

6D p54

8 Fill in the gaps with *a*, *an* or *the*.

1 I've got _an_ old car.
2 I went to _____ cinema at _____
   weekend.
3 What happens at _____ end of
   _____ game?
4 I'd like to buy _____ new hat.
5 This book is about _____ young
   doctor and _____ old woman.
   _____ doctor is rich, but _____
   woman is very poor.

Language Summary Welcome

0.1 ▶ Numbers 0–20 3 p6

0 = zero	7 = seven	14 = fourteen
1 = one	8 = eight	15 = fifteen
2 = two	9 = nine	16 = sixteen
3 = three	10 = ten	17 = seventeen
4 = four	11 = eleven	18 = eighteen
5 = five	12 = twelve	19 = nineteen
6 = six	13 = thirteen	20 = twenty

0.2 ▶ The alphabet 5 p6

Aa Bb Cc Dd Ee Ff Gg Hh Ii

Jj Kk Ll Mm Nn Oo Pp Qq Rr

Ss Tt Uu Vv Ww Xx Yy Zz

TIP • ss = *double s*, A = *capital A*, a = *small a*

0.3 ▶ Things in the classroom 8 p7

a table

a chair

a book

a pencil

a pen

a dictionary

a CD player

a TV

a DVD player

a computer

0.4 ▶ Days of the week 9 p7

Monday	Friday
Tuesday	Saturday
Wednesday	Sunday
Thursday	

0.1 ▶ Introducing yourself 2 p6

Hello, my name's Hassan.

Hi, I'm Olga.

Nice to meet you.

You too.

0.2 ▶ Classroom instructions 4 p6

Open your book.

Look at the photo on page 11.

Do exercise 6 on your own.

Look at the board.

Work in pairs.

Work in groups.

Fill in the gaps.

Compare answers.

Listen and check.

Listen and practise.

Match the words to the pictures.

Ask and answer the questions.

0.3 ▶ Names 6 p7

What's your name?

(My name's/It's) Deniz.

What's your first name?

It's Marcos.

What's your surname?

Fuentes.

How do you spell that?

F–U–E–N–T–E–S.

0.4 ▶ Saying goodbye 10 p7

Goodbye/Bye, Olga.

Goodbye/Bye. See you on Tuesday.

Yes, see you.

Language Summary 1

> **VOCABULARY**

1.1 ▶ Countries, nationalities and languages
1A ▐3▐ p8

countries *I'm from ...*	nationalities *I'm ...*	languages *I speak ...*
Brazil	Brazilian	Portuguese
Australia	Australian	English
Argentina	Argentinian	Spanish
the USA	American	English
Germany	German	German
Italy	Italian	Italian
México	Mexican	Spanish
Russia	Russian	Russian
Egypt	Egyptian	Arabic
the UK	British	English
Spain	Spanish	Spanish
Poland	Polish	Polish
Turkey	Turkish	Turkish
China	Chinese	Chinese
Japan	Japanese	Japanese
France	French	French

1.2 ▶ Jobs 1B ▐3▐ p10

Match the jobs to pictures a–p.

1	*a*	a manager /ˈmænɪdʒə/	9	a musician /mjuːˈzɪʃən/
2		a doctor	10	a teacher
3		an engineer	11	a student
4		a sales assistant	12	a housewife
5		a waiter/a waitress	13	an accountant
6		a cleaner	14	a lawyer /ˈlɔɪə/
7		a police officer	15	a builder
8		an actor/an actress	16	a mechanic

- In the Language Summaries we only show the main stress in words and phrases.

- You can check the phonemic symbols (/æ/, /dʒ/, etc.) on p167.

TIPS • We use *a* or *an* with jobs: *I'm a doctor.* not ~~I'm doctor.~~

• We can also say *I'm unemployed.* not ~~I'm an unemployed.~~ and *I'm retired.* not ~~I'm a retired.~~

• *What do you do?* = *What's your job?*

1.3 ▶ *a* and *an* 1B ▐4▐ p10

- We use **a** with nouns that begin with a **consonant** sound. (The consonants are *b*, *c*, *d*, *f*, etc.): *I'm a student.*

  We use **an** with nouns that begin with a **vowel** sound. (The vowels are *a*, *e*, *i*, *o*, *u*): *He's an actor.*

TIP • We use *a* with nouns that begin with a /j/ sound: *a university* /juːnɪˈvɜːsɪti/.

1.4 ▶ Numbers 20–100 1C ▐1▐ p12

20 = twenty	26 = twenty-six	50 = fifty
21 = twenty-one	27 = twenty-seven	60 = sixty
22 = twenty-two	28 = twenty-eight	70 = seventy
23 = twenty-three	29 = twenty-nine	80 = eighty /ˈeɪti/
24 = twenty-four	30 = thirty /ˈθɜːti/	90 = ninety
25 = twenty-five	40 = forty	100 = a hundred

1.5 ▶ Personal possessions 1D ▐1▐ p14

Do you remember these things? Check on p14.

a diary	an umbrella	a coat	a laptop
a wallet	a bag	a bike/bicycle	a dress
an MP3 player	shoes	a radio	an ID card
a mobile	a camera	a suitcase	false teeth
a watch			

TIP • We can say *a mobile*, *a phone* or *a mobile phone* (US: *a cell*, *a phone* or *a cell phone*).

1.6 ▶ Plurals 1D ▐2▐ p14

singular	plural
	+ -s
a bag	bag**s**
a wallet	wallet**s**
a suitcase	suitcase**s**
	+ -es
a watch	watch**es**
a dress	dress**es**
	-y → -ies
a diary	diar**ies**

singular	irregular plural
a man	men
a woman	women
a child	children
a person	people
a tooth	teeth

TIP • We also add -es to words ending in -s, -sh, -x and -z: *bus* → *buses*, etc.

1.7 ▶ *this, that, these, those*   1D 7 p15

	here ↓	there ↗
singular	this (umbrella)	that (camera)
plural	these (watches)	those (false teeth)

- *This, that, these, those* go **before** *be* in sentences:
  Those are my shoes.
- *This, that, these, those* go **after** *be* in questions:
  Is **that** your bag?

GRAMMAR ▶

1.1 ▶ *be* (1): positive and *Wh-* questions   1A 6 p9

POSITIVE (+)

I'm from Spain.	(= I am)
You're in room 6.	(= you are)
He's from Italy.	(= he is)
She's from Brazil.	(= she is)
It's Carlos Moreno.	(= it is)
We're from Australia.	(= we are)
They're from the UK.	(= they are)

WH- QUESTIONS (?)

Where are you from?
Where's he from?
Where's she from?
What's your name?
What are your names?
Where are they from?

TIPS • *you* and *your* are singular and plural.

• We can write *Where's*, *What's*, etc. but not ~~*Where're*~~, ~~*What're*~~, etc.

1.2 ▶ Subject pronouns and possessive adjectives
1A 9 p9

subject pronouns	I	you	he	she	it	we	they
possessive adjectives	my	your	his	her	its	our	their

TIPS • We use subject pronouns with verbs: *He's a doctor. We live in Paris.*

• We use possessive adjectives with nouns: *My name's Hanif. It's her bag.*

1.3 ▶ *be* (2): negative, *yes/no* questions and short answers   1B 8 p11

NEGATIVE (–)

- We make negatives with *not*.

I'm not a teacher.
You/We/They aren't from the USA. (aren't = are not)
He/She/It isn't famous. (isn't = is not)

YES/NO QUESTIONS (?)	SHORT ANSWERS	
Am I late?	Yes, you are.	No, you aren't.
Are you from Spain?	Yes, I am.	No, I'm not.
Is he/she a musician?	Yes, he/she is.	No, he/she isn't.
Is it Japanese?	Yes, it is.	No, it isn't.
Are we in room 5?	Yes, we/you are.	No, we/you aren't.
Are you from New York?	Yes, we are.	No, we aren't.
Are they French?	Yes, they are.	No, they aren't.

TIPS • We can also make negatives and negative short answers with
's or **'re** + **not**: *She's not famous. You're not from the USA.*
No, you're not. No, she's not, etc.

• We can't say ~~*Yes, you're.*~~ ~~*Yes, I'm,*~~ etc.

REAL WORLD ▶

1.1 ▶ Introducing people   1A 2 p8

Bianca, this is Toshi.

Hello, Toshi. Nice to meet you.

You too.

TIP • When a person says *Nice to meet you.* we can
say *You too.*, *And you.* or *Nice to meet you too.*

1.2 ▶ Asking for personal details
1C 5 p13

What's your surname, please?
What's your first name?
What's your nationality?
What's your address?
What's your postcode?
What's your mobile number?
What's your home number?
What's your email address?

TIPS • We can say *surname* or *last name*.

• In phone numbers 0 = *oh* or *zero* and 11 = *double one*.

• We can say *What's your home number?* or *What's
your landline (number)?*

• In email addresses we say: . = *dot*, @ = *at*,
A = *capital A*.

• *postcode* (UK) = *zip code* (US)

• We say *How old are you?* to ask about age: **A** *How
old are you?* **B** *I'm fifty.* not ~~*I have fifty.*~~ or ~~*I'm fifty years.*~~

• If you're not married, you can say you're **single**:
A *Are you married?* **B** *No, I'm single.*

• We say *years old* for things: *My bike's ten years old.*
not ~~*My bike's ten.*~~

1.3 ▶ Asking people to repeat things
1C 7 p13

I'm sorry?
Could you say that again, please?
Could you repeat that, please?

Language Summary 2

VOCABULARY

2.1 ▶ Adjectives (1)

2A 1 p16

Match the adjectives to pictures a–n.

1	new ☐	old
2	good ☐	bad
3	cheap ☐	expensive
4	beautiful ☐	ugly
5	easy ☐	difficult
6	big ☐	small
7	early ☐	late
8	fast ☐	slow
9	young ☐	old
10	right ☐	wrong
11	nice ☐m☐	
12	great ☐	
13	important ☐	
14	favourite ☐	

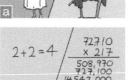
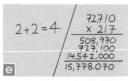

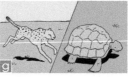

2.2 ▶ Adjective word order and *very*

2A 2 p16

- We put adjectives **after** the verb *be*: *She's **late**.*
- We put adjectives **before** a noun: *It's a **small** bag.*
- We put *very* **before** adjectives: *It's a **very** difficult question.*
- Adjectives **aren't** plural with plural nouns: *Those are my **new** shoes.*

2.3 ▶ Family 2B 2 p18

♂ **male**	♀ **female**	⚥ **male and female**
father (dad)	mother (mum)	parents
son /sʌn/	daughter /'dɔːtə/	children (kids)
brother /'brʌðə/	sister	–
husband	wife (plural: wives)	–
grandfather	grandmother	grandparents
grandson	granddaughter	grandchildren
uncle	aunt /ɑːnt/	–
cousin /'kʌzən/	cousin	cousins

TIPS • *parents* = mother and father only; *relatives* = all the people in your family.

• *brothers* = men/boys only. We ask: *How many brothers and sisters have you got?*

• *a boyfriend/girlfriend* = a man/woman you have a romantic relationship with.

• We use **How many** (+ noun) to ask about a number: *How many children have you got?*

• *Dad, mum* and *kids* are informal words.

2.4 ▶ Time words 2C 1 p20

60 **seconds** = 1 **minute** /'mɪnɪt/   7 days = 1 **week**
60 minutes = 1 **hour**   12 **months** = 1 **year**
24 hours = 1 **day**

TIP • We say *two and a half hours* not ~~two hours and a half~~.

2.5 ▶ Things in a house 2D 1 p22

Match the words to a–l in the picture.

1 ☐	a mirror	5 ☐	a door	9 ☐	a plant			
2 ☐	a desk	6 ☐	a bookcase	10 ☐	a coffee table			
3 ☐	a sofa	7 ☐	a window	11 ☐h☐	a lamp			
4 ☐	a carpet	8 ☐	the floor	12 ☐	curtains			

2.6 ▸ **Prepositions of place** 2D **2** p22

in · on · by

under · behind · in front of

GRAMMAR

2.1 ▸ *have got*: **positive and negative** 2A **5** p16

POSITIVE (+)	NEGATIVE (–)
I've got (= I have got)	I haven't got (= I have not got)
you've got	you haven't got
he's got (= he has got)	he hasn't got (= he has not got)
she's got	she hasn't got
it's got	it hasn't got
we've got	we haven't got
they've got	they haven't got

TIP • We use *any* with plural nouns in negatives: *He hasn't got any DVDs.*

2.2 ▸ *have got*: **questions and short answers**
2A **10** p17

YES/NO QUESTIONS (?)	SHORT ANSWERS	
Have I got any letters today?	Yes, you have.	No, you haven't.
Have you got a camera?	Yes, I have.	No, I haven't.
Has he got a DVD player?	Yes, he has.	No, he hasn't.
Has she got a DVD player?	Yes, she has.	No, she hasn't.
Has it got a DVD player?	Yes, it has.	No, it hasn't.
Have we got any CDs?	Yes, we/you have.	No, we/you haven't.
Have they got any cheap TVs?	Yes, they have.	No, they haven't.

TIPS • We use *any* with plural nouns in *yes/no* questions:
Have you got any DVDs?

• We don't use *got* in short answers:
Yes, I have. not ~~Yes, I have got~~.

WH- QUESTIONS

What have you got in your bag?
What has he/she got in his/her bag?

2.3 ▸ **Possessive 's** 2B **5** p19

• We use a name + **'s** (*Pam's*, etc.) or a noun + **'s**
(*husband's*, etc.) for the possessive:
Jill is Pam's sister.   My husband's name is Nick.

TIPS • For plural nouns, we write **s'**:
My parents' names are Mary and Ben.

• *'s* can mean the possessive, *is* or *has*:
Ben is Pam's father. (*'s* = possessive)
Jill's her sister. (*'s* = is)
She's got one brother. (*'s* = has)

• We use *Whose* to ask which person/people a thing
belongs to: **A** *Whose mobile phone is it?* **B** *It's Nick's.*

REAL WORLD

2.1 ▸ **Telling the time** 2C **2** **3** p20

one o'clock / one · five past two / two oh five · ten past three / three ten

quarter past four / four fifteen · twenty past five / five twenty · twenty-five past six / six twenty-five

half past seven / seven thirty · twenty-five to eight / seven thirty-five · twenty to nine / eight forty

quarter to ten / nine forty-five · ten to eleven / ten fifty · five to twelve / eleven fifty-five

TIPS • We can say *quarter past/to six* or **a** *quarter past/to six*. We don't say ~~fifteen past six~~.

• For other times, we say *minutes*: *nineteen minutes past six* not ~~nineteen past six~~.

2.2 ► Talking about the time   2C 5 p20

QUESTIONS ABOUT THE TIME

What time is it? | It's one o'clock.

What's the time, please? | It's about half past seven.

Excuse me. Have you got the time, please? | Yes, it's four fifteen.

PREPOSITIONS OF TIME

- We use **at** for times: *My English class is at ten.*
- We use **from … to** for length of time: *My son's class is from seven to nine thirty.*

TIP • a.m. = 0.00–12.00   midday/noon = 12.00
p.m. = 12.00–24.00   midnight = 24.00

2.3 ► Saying prices   2C 8 p21

£20 = twenty pounds
£7.50 = seven pounds fifty
40p = forty p /pi:/
£29.99 = twenty-nine ninety-nine

€9 = nine euros /ˈjʊərəʊz/
€6.50 = six euros fifty
$35 = thirty-five dollars
50c = fifty cents /sents/

2.4 ► Buying tickets at the cinema   2C 11 p21

CUSTOMER

Can I have (two) tickets for (*The Brothers*), please?

(Two) tickets for (*A New Day*), please. One adult and one child.

How much is that?
How much are the tickets?

Here you are. What time is the film?

Right. Thanks a lot.
Thank you very much.

TICKET SELLER

Yes, of course.

That's (£23), please.
(£11.50) for adults and (£8.45) for children. So that's (£19.95), please.

It starts at (seven fifteen).
It starts in (two minutes).

You're welcome. Enjoy the film.

TIPS • We say *How much **is** + this, that* or a singular noun:
How much is that? How much is the exhibition?

• We say *How much **are** + these, those* or a plural noun:
How much are these? How much are the tickets?

Language Summary 3

VOCABULARY ►

3.1 ► Daily routines   3A 1 p24

Match the words/phrases to pictures a–o.

1 ☐ get up
2 ☐ go to bed
3 ☐ have breakfast /ˈbrekfəst/
4 ☐ have lunch
5 ☐ have dinner
6 ☐ start work /wɜːk/
7 ☐ start classes
8 ☐ finish work

9 ☐ finish classes
10 ☐ leave home
11 ☐ get home
12 g work
13 h study
14 ☐ sleep
15 ☐ live

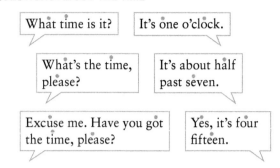

3.2 ▶ Free time activities (1)   3B 1 p26

Match the phrases to pictures a–l.

1	f stay in	7	go shopping
2	go out (a lot)	8	phone friends/my family
3	eat out	9	visit friends/my family
4	go for a drink	10	have coffee with friends
5	go to the cinema	11	do (a lot of) sport
6	go to concerts	12	watch (a lot of) TV/DVDs

TIPS • We say: *Do you want to go for a drink?* not ~~Do you want to drink something?~~

• We can say **do** sport or **play** sport: *I play sport at the weekend.*

• We can say **a lot of** + noun or **lots of** + noun: *I do a lot of sport. I watch lots of DVDs.*

• *go to the cinema* (UK) = *go to the movies* (US)

3.3 ▶ Time phrases with *on, in, at, every*   3B 9 p27

on	in	at	every
+ day	**+ part of the day**	**+ time**	week
Saturday	the morning	nine o'clock	day
Mondays	the afternoon	half past three	month
Monday mornings	the evening		night
Sunday afternoon		night	morning
	the week	the weekend	Sunday afternoon

TIPS • We can use the singular or plural of days, parts of the day and *the weekend* to talk about routines: *I stay in on Monday/Mondays. I go out in the evening/evenings. I work at the weekend/weekends.*

• We don't use a plural with *every*: *every week* not ~~every weeks~~.

• We say **in** the morning/afternoon/evening but **at** night.

3.4 ▶ Months   3C 3 p28

January   July
February   August
March   September
April   October
May   November
June   December

TIP • We use *in* with months: *My birthday's in December.*

3.5 ▶ Dates   3C 4 p28

1st	first	17th	seventeenth
2nd	second	18th	eighteenth
3rd	third	19th	nineteenth
4th	fourth	20th	twentieth
5th	fifth	21st	twenty-first
6th	sixth	22nd	twenty-second
7th	seventh	23rd	twenty-third
8th	eighth	24th	twenty-fourth
9th	ninth	25th	twenty-fifth
10th	tenth	26th	twenty-sixth
11th	eleventh	27th	twenty-seventh
12th	twelfth	28th	twenty-eighth
13th	thirteenth	29th	twenty-ninth
14th	fourteenth	30th	thirtieth
15th	fifteenth	31st	thirty-first
16th	sixteenth		

3.6 ▶ Frequency adverbs   3D 1 p30

always   often   hardly ever
    usually   sometimes   never

100%   0%

3.7 ▶ Word order of frequency adverbs   3D 4 p30

● Frequency adverbs go **after** the verb *be*:
*I'm **always** happy and I have a lot of energy.*

● Frequency adverbs go **before** other verbs:
*I **sometimes** get up before 9 a.m.*

TIPS • We can use *always*, *usually* and *often* with negative verb forms: *I **don't often** eat out.*

• We can't use *sometimes*, *hardly ever* or *never* with negative verb forms: ~~We don't **sometimes** watch TV.~~

3.1 ▶ Present Simple (1): positive (*I/you/we/they*)   3A 4 p24

- We use the Present Simple to talk about daily routines.
- The Present Simple positive is the same for *I, you, we* and *they*.

I **get up** at 4.30 in the morning.
You **get up** very early.
We **start** work at about 7.00.
They **have** an hour for lunch.

3.2 ▶ Present Simple (1): *Wh-* questions (*I/you/we/they*)   3A 9 p25

question word	auxiliary	subject	infinitive	
What time	do	you	get up?	
When	do	you	have	lunch?
When	do	you	finish	work?
What time	do	you	get	home?
Where	do	you	have	dinner?

TIP • Present Simple questions are the same for *I, you, we* and *they*: *Who do **I** ask? When do **we** start classes? What time do **they** have lunch?*

3.3 ▶ Present Simple (2): negative (*I/you/we/they*)   3B 4 p26

- In Present Simple negative sentences with *I, you, we* and *they* we use:
  subject + don't (= do not) + **infinitive**

subject	auxiliary	infinitive	
I	don't	go out	on Saturday evening.
You	don't	work	in this office.
We	don't	stay in	at the weekend.
They	don't	watch	TV in the day.

3.4 ▶ Present Simple (2): *yes/no* questions and short answers (*I/you/we/they*)   3B 6 p27

YES/NO QUESTIONS (?)				SHORT ANSWERS
auxiliary	subject	infinitive		
Do	you	eat out	a lot?	Yes, I do. No, I don't.
Do	you	go	to concerts?	Yes, we do. No, we don't.
Do	they	watch	TV a lot?	Yes, they do. No, they don't.

3.5 ▶ Subject and object pronouns   3D 6 p31

subject pronouns	I	you	he	she	it	we	they
object pronouns	me	you	him	her	it	us	them

TIP • In positive and negative sentences, subject pronouns go **before** the verb and object pronouns go **after** the verb: *I often see him on Saturday. They don't usually call her in the morning.*

REAL WORLD

3.1 ▶ Phrases for special days   3C 2 p28

a birthday /ˈbɜːθdeɪ/ — Happy birthday!

a wedding
the birth of a new baby — Congratulations!

a New Year's Eve party — Happy New Year!

a wedding anniversary — Happy anniversary!

3.2 ▶ Talking about days and dates   3C 5 p28

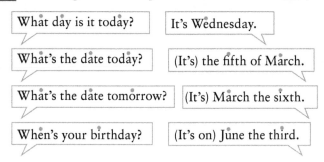

What day is it today? — It's Wednesday.

What's the date today? — (It's) the fifth of March.

What's the date tomorrow? — (It's) March the sixth.

When's your birthday? — (It's on) June the third.

TIPS • We say: **the fifth of** March or March **the fifth**. We write: *5th March* or *March 5th*.

• We use **on** with dates: *My birthday's on December 30th.*

• In the UK, *3.7.17 = 3rd July 2017* (day/month/year).
In the USA, *3.7.17 = 7th March 2017* (month/day/year).

3.3 ▶ Suggestions   3C 9 p29

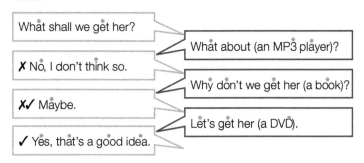

What shall we get her?

✗ No, I don't think so.

✗✓ Maybe.

✓ Yes, that's a good idea.

What about (an MP3 player)?

Why don't we get her (a book)?

Let's get her (a DVD).

TIPS • We can say **get** or **buy**: *What shall we get/buy her?*

• We use the infinitive after *What shall we … ?* and *Let's … : What shall we **do** tonight? Let's **go** to the cinema.*

Language Summary 4

VOCABULARY

4.1 ▶ Free time activities (2)

4A 1 p32

Match the phrases to pictures a–l.

1. [ ] take photos
2. [ ] go to the gym
3. [ ] watch sport on TV
4. [ ] play video games
5. [ ] play tennis
6. [ ] read books or magazines
7. [ ] go cycling
8. [ ] go swimming
9. [ ] go running
10. [ ] go clubbing
11. [ ] listen to music
12. [ ] listen to the radio

TIPS • We can say *play video games* or *play computer games*.

• *go cycling* (UK) = *go biking* (US)

4.2 ▶ Things you like and don't like   4B 1 p34

Match the words/phrases to pictures a–o.

1. [ ] reading
2. [ ] football
3. [ ] travelling
4. [ ] cats
5. [ ] shopping for clothes
6. [ ] video games
7. [ ] animals
8. [ ] dancing
9. [ ] cooking
10. [ ] dance music
11. [ ] rock music
12. [ ] jazz
13. [ ] Italian food
14. [ ] Chinese food
15. [ ] fast food

4.3 ▶ *like/love/hate*   4B 2 p34

I love ...

I really like ...

I like ...

I quite like ...

... is/are OK.

I don't like ...

I hate ...

4.4 ▶ Verb+*ing*   4B 3 p34

verb + verb+*ing*	verb + noun
I love **reading**.	I love **rock music**.
I really like **travelling**.	I like **books**.
I don't like **shopping** for clothes.	I quite like **Italian food**.
I hate **cooking**.	I don't like **video games**.

TIPS • We use *enjoy* + verb+*ing* to say we like doing something: *I enjoy travelling.*

• We don't use *the* to talk about things we like/don't like in general: *I love books.* (= books in general). *He doesn't like cats.* (= cats in general).

• We often use *very much* with *like*. We put it after the noun or verb+*ing*: *I like reading very much.* not *I like very much reading.*

4.5 ▶ Food and drink (1) 4C 2 p36

a pizza

a burger and chips
(US: *French fries*)

a cheeseburger
and chips

a glass of
white wine

a bottle of
red wine

a bottle
of beer

a bottle of
still mineral
water

a bottle of
sparkling
mineral
water

a tuna salad

a chicken salad

a mixed salad

an egg mayonnaise
sandwich

a cheese and tomato
sandwich

apple pie with cream

fruit salad

vanilla, strawberry,
chocolate ice cream

tea and coffee

4.6 ▶ Food and drink (2) 4D 1 p38

Match the words to pictures a–y.

1	☐	biscuits /ˈbɪskɪts/	14	☐	cheese
2	☐	milk	15	☐	a banana
3	☐	an apple	16	☐	orange juice
4	☐	rice	17	☐	a croissant /ˈkwæsɒ/
5	☐	yogurt /ˈjɒgət/	18	☐	tea
6	☐	sugar	19	☐	jam
7	☐	toast	20	☐	meat
8	☐	bread	21	☐	fruit
9	☐	fish	22	☐	cereal
10	☐	eggs	23	☐	olives
11	☐	coffee	24	☐	tomatoes
12	☐	sausages /ˈsɒsɪdʒɪz/	25	☐	vegetables /ˈvedʒtəblz/
13	☐	soup			

TIPS • *biscuits* (UK) = *cookies* (US)

• *jam* (UK) = *jelly* (US)

4.7 ▶ Countable and uncountable nouns 4D 5 p38

COUNTABLE NOUNS

● Countable nouns have a plural form: *biscuits, apples*.

● We use *a* or *an* with singular countable nouns: ***a** biscuit, **an** apple*.

● We don't use *a* or *an* with plural countable nouns:
biscuits not ***a** biscuits, apples* not ***an** apples*.

UNCOUNTABLE NOUNS

● Uncountable nouns aren't usually plural:
milk not ~~milks~~, *rice* not ~~rices~~.

● We don't use *a* or *an* with uncountable nouns:
milk not ~~**a** milk~~, *rice* not ~~**a** rice~~.

TIP • Some nouns can be countable and uncountable: *I like coffee.* (uncountable = coffee in general) *Can I have a coffee, please?*
(countable = a cup of coffee)

136 ▶

4.1 ▶ Present Simple (3): positive and negative (*he/she/it*) 4A [5] p32

POSITIVE (+)

● In Present Simple positive sentences with *he*, *she* and *it* we add *-s* or *-es* to the infinitive.

He **plays** video games.   She **emails** him every day.
He **watches** lots of DVDs.   It **starts** at ten o'clock..

TIP • The verb *have* is irregular. We say *he/she/it* **has**, not *he/she/it* **haves**: *He has tennis lessons every week.*

NEGATIVE (–)

● In Present Simple negative sentences with *he*, *she* and *it* we use:

subject + doesn't (= does not) + **infinitive**

subject	auxiliary	infinitive	
He	doesn't	like	the weather.
She	doesn't	talk	to him very often.
It	doesn't	start	at ten thirty.

4.2 ▶ Present Simple (3) positive: spelling rules (*he/she/it*) 4A [6] p33

spelling rule	examples
most verbs: add *-s*	play**s** write**s** phone**s** get**s** start**s** live**s**
verbs ending in *-ch*, *-sh*, *-s*, *-ss*, *-x* or *-z*: add *-es*	watch**es** /ˈwɒtʃɪz/ finish**es** /ˈfɪnɪʃɪz/
verbs ending in consonant + *y*: *-y* → *-ies*	stud**ies**
the verbs *go* and *do*: add *-es*	go**es** do**es** /dʌz/
the verb *have* is irregular	**has**

4.3 ▶ Present Simple (4): questions and short answers (*he/she/it*) 4B [7] p35

QUESTIONS (?)

question word	auxiliary	subject	infinitive	
What	does	she	do	in her free time?
	Does	she	watch	TV a lot?
	Does	she	like	films?
What (music)	does	she	like?	

● Present Simple questions are the same for *he*, *she* and *it*:
*Where does **he** live? What time does **it** start?*
*Does **she** like football? Does **it** start at nine o'clock?*

TIP • We sometimes use a noun with some question words (*What, How many*, etc.): *What **music** do you like? How many **children** have you got?*

SHORT ANSWERS

Yes, he does.	No, he doesn't.
Yes, she does.	No, she doesn't.
Yes, it does.	No, it doesn't.

TIPS • We use **do** in questions with *I*, *you*, *we* and *they*. We use **does** in questions with *he*, *she* and *it*.

● We don't repeat the verb in short answers:
Yes, she does. not *Yes, she likes.*
No, she doesn't. not *No, she doesn't like.*

4.4 ▶ *have* or *have got*? 4B [7] p35

● We can use **have** or **have got** to talk about possessions and family:
She's got two dogs. = She has two dogs.
I haven't got any children. = I don't have any children.
Have you got a car? = Do you have a car?

● We can only use **have** to talk about meals and other activities:
I don't have breakfast. not *I haven't **got** breakfast.*
We often have coffee with friends. not *We often have **got** coffee with friends.*
Do you want to have a game of tennis? not *Do you want to have **got** a game of tennis?*

REAL WORLD

4.1 ▶ Requests and offers 4C [7] p37

REQUESTS

● We use **I'd/We'd like …** and **Can I/we have … ?** for requests (we want something).

> I'd/We'd like a bottle of mineral water, please.

> Can I/we have the bill, please?

OFFERS

● We use **Would you like … ?** for offers (we want to give something or help someone).

> Would you like to order now?

> What would you like to drink?

TIPS • *I'd like = I would like; We'd like = We would like.*

• We use a noun after *Can I/we have … ?*: *Can I have **the bill**, please?*

• We use a noun or the infinitive with *to* after *Would you like … ?* and *I'd/We'd like …* : *Would you like **a dessert**? I'd like **to order** now, please.*

• *the bill* (UK) = *the check* (US)

Language Summary 5

VOCABULARY

5.1 ▶ Adjectives (2) 5A **1** p40

Match these pairs of words to pictures a–j.

1	hot ☐	cold
2	noisy ☐	quiet
3	well ☐	ill
4	short ☐	tall
5	lucky ☐	unlucky
6	different ☐	the same
7	happy ☐	unhappy
8	boring ☐	interesting
9	friendly ☐	unfriendly
10	terrible/awful ☐	fantastic/amazing/wonderful

5.3 ▶ Life events 5B **1** p42

leave school/university	**have** children/a dream
meet my husband/my wife	**move** house/to a different country
get married/divorced	**study** English/physics
make a film/a lot of money	**write** a book/a letter
become a film director/famous	**win** an Oscar/the lottery

TIP • *a film* (UK) = *a movie* (US)

5.4 ▶ Weekend activities 5C **1** p44

go for a walk	**go away** for the weekend
go for a run	**go away** for a couple of days
clean the car	**have** a great time
clean the house	**have** a bad cold
do the washing	**go to** a party
do your homework	**go to** your parents' house for lunch
write an email	**stay** with friends
write a report	**stay** at home all weekend

TIP • *do the washing* (UK) = *do the laundry* (US)

5.5 ▶ Adjectives (3)

5D **1** p46

Match these adjectives to pictures a–l.

1	☐	bored /bɔːd/
2	☐	crowded
3	*h*	busy /ˈbɪzi/
4	☐	comfortable
5	☐	dirty
6	☐	rich
7	☐	dangerous
8	☐	clean
9	☐	poor
10	☐	excited
11	*l*	safe
12	☐	empty

very bad   very good

5.2 ▶ Years 5A **9** p41

1835 = eighteen thirty-five
1900 = nineteen hundred
1990 = nineteen ninety
2000 = two thousand
2005 = two thousand and five
2018 = twenty eighteen

TIPS • We use *in* with years: *I was born **in** 1990.*

• 2000–2009 = *two thousand, two thousand and one, two thousand and two*, etc.

• 2010–2099 = *twenty ten, twenty eleven*, etc.

5.6 ▶ Adjectives with *very, really, quite, too* 5D **4** p47

It's **quite** big.   It's **very/really** big.   It's **too** big.

• *Too* has a negative meaning. It means *more than you want*.

• *Very, really, quite* and *too* come **after** the verb *be* and **before** adjectives:
*I was **really** excited. The restaurant was **quite** dirty.*

TIP • We don't use *too* to mean *very very*: *She's really happy.* not ~~She's too happy~~.

5.1 ▶ Past Simple (1): *be* (positive and negative)   5A **3** p40

POSITIVE (+)	NEGATIVE (−)
I was	I wasn't (= was not)
you/we/they were	you/we/they weren't (= were not)
he/she/it was	he/she/it wasn't

It was a fantastic party!
About thirty people were here.
Robert wasn't here because he was ill.
My two brothers weren't here.

5.2 ▶ Past Simple (1): *be* (questions and short answers)   5A **7** p41

QUESTIONS (?)

question word	*was/were*	subject	
When	was	Albert's 13th birthday?	
Where	was	the party?	
	Were	his friends	there?
	Was	the food	good?
Where	were	his grandparents?	

SHORT ANSWERS

Yes, I/he/she/it was.	No, I/he/she/it wasn't.
Yes, you/we/they were.	No, you/we/they weren't.

WAS BORN/WERE BORN

| When were you born? | I was born in 1940. |
| Where was Matt born? | He was born in Liverpool. |

TIP • We say *I was born in 1940.* not ~~I born in 1940.~~

5.3 ▶ Past Simple (2): regular and irregular verbs (positive)   5B **4** p42

● We use the Past Simple to talk about the past. We know when these things happened.

● The Past Simple positive is the same for all subjects (*I*, *you*, *he*, *she*, *it*, *we*, *they*).

regular verbs: spelling rule	examples	
most regular verbs: add -*ed*	wanted started	worked visited
regular verbs ending in -*e*: add -*d*	moved	loved
regular verbs ending in consonant + *y*: -*y* → -*i* and add -*ed*	studied	married
regular verbs ending in consonant + vowel + consonant: double the last consonant	stopped	

TIP • There are no rules for **irregular verbs**. There is an Irregular Verb List on p167.

5.4 ▶ Past Simple (2): *Wh-* questions   5B **9** p43

● Past Simple questions are the same for all subjects (*I*, *you*, *he*, *she*, *it*, *we*, *they*).

question word	auxiliary	subject	infinitive	
What	did	James	study	at university?
When	did	he	make	*Terminator 2*?
Which (film)	did	he	make	in 3D in 2009?
Who	did	he	marry	in 1997?

TIP • Notice the difference between these questions:
*Where **do** you live?* (Present Simple)
*Where **did** you live?* (Past Simple).

REAL WORLD

5.1 ▶ Showing interest   5C **4** p45

I'm happy for you.	I'm sorry for you.	I'm surprised.	I'm not surprised.
Oh, nice. Oh, great!	Oh, dear. What a shame.	Wow! Really? You're joking!	Oh, right.

5.2 ▶ Asking follow-up questions   5C **6** p45

QUESTIONS YOU CAN ASK SOMEONE WHO ...

... WAS ILL AT THE WEEKEND	... STAYED AT HOME	... WENT TO THE CINEMA	... WENT AWAY FOR THE WEEKEND
What was wrong? Are you OK now?	What did you do?	What did you see? What was it like? Who did you go with?	What was it like? Where did you go? Who did you go with? Where did you stay?

Language Summary 6

VOCABULARY

6.1 ▶ The internet   6A 1 p48

use the internet	**go** online
send emails	**have** a favourite website
get emails	**chat** to your friends online
read a blog	**have** WiFi
download videos or music	**use** a search engine

TIPS • We can say *get emails* or *receive emails*.

• We *download music* or *videos* **onto** *a computer/laptop*. The opposite of *download* is *upload*.

• We can say *chat* **to** *someone* or *chat* **with** *someone*.

• Google is a popular *search engine*. We can also use *google* as a verb: *Why don't you google it?*

• *Email, download, video, chat* and *blog* can be nouns or verbs: *I email my brother a lot. She blogs every day.*

6.2 ▶ Mobile phones and TVs   6B 1 p50

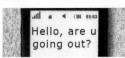

send/get a text

charge your phone

GPS

a channel

a TV programme

a battery

an app

turn on

turn off

record

TIPS • You can *get* or *receive a text. Text* is also a regular verb: *He texted me yesterday.*

• You use *a charger* to charge your mobile phone.

• *TV programme* (UK) = *TV show* (US)

6.3 ▶ Past time phrases   6B 2 p50

AGO

• We use **ago** to talk about a time in the past. We use it with the Past Simple: *I met him two years ago.* (= two years before now).

LAST

• We use **last** to say the day, week, etc. in the past nearest to now: *I met him last Friday.* (= the Friday before now).

• We use **last** with **days** (*last Monday*), **months** (*last March*) and in these phrases: *last night, last week, last weekend, last month, last year, last century.*

TIPS • We say *last night*, but *yesterday morning/afternoon/ evening* not ~~last morning~~, etc.

• We don't use a preposition with *last*: *last year* not ~~in last year~~.

IN

• We use **in** with **years** (*in 1986*) and **months** (*in May*).

• We use **in the** with **decades** (*in the nineties*) and **centuries** (*in the eighteenth century*).

TIPS • We can use **on** with **days** (*on Monday*) to mean *last*: *I met him on Monday.* = *I met him last Monday.*

• *the day before yesterday* = two days ago

6.4 ▶ Verbs from news stories   6C 2 p52

REGULAR VERBS

damage /'dæmidʒ/

sail

die

receive

crash

save

IRREGULAR VERBS

buy (bought /bɔːt/)

lose /luːz/ (lost)

find (found)

put (put)

say (said /sed/)

tell (told)

6.5 ▶ Articles: *a, an* and *the*   6D 4 p55

• We use **the** when we know which thing, person, place, etc. because there is only one: *People call him* **the father** *of video games.*

• We use **a** or **an** to talk about things or people for the first time: *The story always has* **a hero***,* **a princess** *and* **a villain***.*

• We use **the** to talk about a person or a thing for the second, third, etc. time: **The villain** *wants to marry* **the princess***.*

TIPS • We use *the* in some fixed phrases: *at* **the** *weekend, in* **the** *evening, go to* **the** *cinema*, etc.

• We also use *the* with *first, second, third*, etc.: *Shigeru designed* **the** *first Mario Brothers game in 1983.*

6.1 ▸ Past Simple (3): negative   6A 3 p48

- To make the Past Simple negative of *be*, we use *wasn't* or *weren't* (see GRAMMAR 5.1):
  *In the early days of the internet, search engines **weren't** very good and it **wasn't** easy for people to find the information they wanted.*

- To make the Past Simple negative of all other verbs, we use:
  subject + didn't (= did not) + **infinitive**

subject	auxiliary	infinitive	
They	didn't	like	each other at first.
They	didn't	finish	their course.
They	didn't	have	any money.

TIP • We use *didn't* for all subjects (*I, you, he, she, it, we, they*):
I didn't go out last night.
He didn't call me yesterday.

6.2 ▸ Past Simple (3): *yes/no* questions and short answers   6A 8 p49

YES/NO QUESTIONS (?)

auxiliary	subject	infinitive	
Did	you	go	to the cinema last week?
Did	Sergey	leave	Russia in 1978?
Did	he	go	to Maryland University?
Did	his parents	teach	computer science?

SHORT ANSWERS

Yes, I did.	No, I didn't.
Yes, you did.	No, you didn't.
Yes, he/she/it did.	No, he/she/it didn't.
Yes, we did.	No, we didn't.
Yes, they did.	No, they didn't.

TIP • Past Simple *yes/no* questions and short answers are the same for all subjects (*I, you, he, she, it, we, they*):
A *Did you go shopping last weekend?*
B *Yes, I did./No, I didn't.*

6.3 ▸ *can/can't; could/couldn't*   6B 4 p51

POSITIVE (+)

- We use ***can*** + **infinitive** to say that something is possible in the present.
  You can choose from hundreds of TV channels.
  You can watch TV programmes online.

- We use ***could*** + **infinitive** to say that something was possible in the past.
  In the seventies you could only get three channels.
  I could watch all my favourite programmes in colour!

NEGATIVE (–)

- The negative of *can* is ***can't*** (= *cannot*).
  My son and daughter can't understand how people lived without them.
  I can't explain this to my kids.

- The negative of *could* is ***couldn't*** (= *could not*).
  You couldn't record TV programmes.
  You couldn't watch TV all night.

TIPS • *Can/can't* and *could/couldn't* are the same for all subjects (*I, you, he, she, it, we, they*).

• We sometimes use *you* to mean 'people in general': *You could only get three channels. = People could only get three channels.*

YES/NO QUESTIONS (?)	SHORT ANSWERS
Can you watch TV online?	Yes, you can. No, you can't.
Could you record programmes in 1974?	Yes, you could. No, you couldn't.

- *Yes/No* questions and short answers with *can/could* are the same for all subjects (*I, you, he, she, it, we, they*):
  A *Can he/she download videos?* **B** *Yes, he/she can.*
  A *Could they record programmes?* **B** *No, they couldn't.*

- We can also use question words (*What, How many*, etc.) with *can/could*: *How many channels can/could you get?*

TIPS • We don't use *do, does* or *did* in questions with *can/could*: *Can you watch TV online?* not *Do you can watch TV online?*.

• We can also use *can/could* for ability in the present and the past: *My sister can speak Russian. How many languages could your grandfather speak?*

• We also use *can* for requests (*Can you help me?*) and offers (*Can I help you?*).

6.1 ▸ Talking about the news   6C 9 p53

- To start a conversation about the news, we can say:

> Did you hear about that train crash?

> No, where was it?

> Did you read about the eighty-year-old couple and their boat?

> No, what happened?

- To respond to good, bad and surprising news, we can say:

good news	bad news	surprising news
Oh, that's good.	Oh no, that's terrible. Yes, isn't it awful? Oh, dear. Are they OK?	Really? You're joking!

TIP • *News* is a singular noun. We say: *The news is terrible.* not *The news are terrible.*

Audio and Video Scripts

CD1 4

Do exercise 6 on your own. | Listen and practise. | Look at the board. | Listen and check. | Work in pairs. | Match the words to the pictures. | Fill in the gaps. | Ask and answer the questions. | Work in groups. | Look at the photo on page 11. | Compare answers. | Open your book.

CD1 6

class | photo | please | listen | nineteen

CD1 7

MARCOS Hello. Sorry I'm late.
TEACHER No problem. What's your first name?
M It's Marcos.
T What's your surname?
M Fuentes.
T How do you spell that?
M F–U–E–N–T–E–S.
T Welcome to the class, Marcos.
M Thank you.

CD1 8

A CAMILLE Hello, is this the English class?
 TEACHER Yes, it is.
C Oh, good. Sorry I'm late!
T No problem. What's your first name?
C Camille.
T How do you spell that?
C C–A–M–I–double L–E.
T And what's your surname?
C It's Laurent.
T And how do you spell that?
C L–A–U–R–E–N–T.
T Thanks, Camille. Welcome to the class.

B BARTEK Hello, sorry I'm late.
 TEACHER No problem. What's your name?
B My name's Bartek.
T How do you spell that, please?
B B–A–R–T–E–K.
T And what's your surname?
B Kowalski.
T OK. And how do you spell that?
B K–O–W–A–L–S–K–I.
T Thanks. Welcome to the class, Bartek.
B Thank you.

CD1 11

ANSWER Tuesday

CD1 15

ANSWERS 3 Spain 4 Australia 5 Italy, Brazil, the UK

CD1 18

A A What's your phone number?
B Er … wait a minute … it's 01221 960744.
A 01221 960744?
B Yes, that's right.

B A What's Tina's mobile number?
B It's 07906 394896.
A 07906 … er …
B 394896.

C A What's the phone number of your hotel?
B It's 0119 498 0691. I'm in room 302.
A OK, thanks.

D A What's your number in Australia?
B It's 0061 02 9967 2315.
A So that's 0061 … 02 …
B … 9967 2315.
A OK. Thanks.

CD1 20

ANSWERS 1 engineer 2 doctor 3 musician 4 police officer 5 accountant

CD1 21

I'm not a teacher. | We aren't from the USA. | She isn't famous. | Are you from Spain? | Yes, I am. | No, I'm not. | Is she a musician? | Yes, she is. | No, she isn't. | Are you from New York? | Yes, we are. | No, we aren't.

CD1 23

forty | seventeen | eighty | sixty | eighteen | fourteen | sixteen | seventy

VIDEO 1 CD1 26

WOMAN Right, first I need some personal details. What's your surname, please?
P It's Whatling.
W And how do you spell that?
P W–H–A–T–L–I–N–G.
W OK, thanks. What's your first name?
P Paul.
W And what's your nationality?
P I'm British.
W OK. What's your address?
P It's 29 Elmore Road, Bristol.
W How do you spell Elmore?
P E–L–M–O–R–E.
W And what's your postcode?
P BS13 6QT.
W I'm sorry?
P BS13 6QT.
W Great, thanks a lot. What's your mobile number?
P 07969 831016.
W 07969 …
P … 831016.
W OK. And what's your home number?
P It's 0117 480 6544.
W Could you say that again, please?
P 0117 480 6544.
W Right. And the last question … what's your email address?
P It's paul ninety-nine at webmail dot com.
W Could you repeat that, please?
P Yes, paul ninety-nine at webmail dot com.

W OK, thanks a lot. Now, what type of car would you like?

CD1 30

this → What's this? → What's this in English? | that → What's that? → What's that in English? | these → What are these? → What are these in English? | those → What are those?

CD1 32

British | teacher | thirty | mobile | Japan | address | thirteen | Brazil | bicycle | manager | Germany | Mexican | computer | musician | umbrella | mechanic | seventeen | engineer | Japanese | unemployed

CD1 34

I've got an old car. | You've got a new mobile. | He's got a big TV. | She's got a new bicycle. | We've got a beautiful cat. | They've got an old DVD player. | I haven't got a laptop. | We haven't got a car. | He hasn't got a diary.

CD1 35

INTERVIEWER Hello. Have you got time to answer some questions? It's a product survey about computers, cameras, TVs, that sort of thing.
MARY Yes, OK.
ALAN Sure.
I Oh, good. Thanks. Right, first question. Have you got a laptop?
A No, I haven't, but I've got an old computer.
I And you, madam? Have you got a laptop?
M Yes, I have, but it's not very good.
I Thanks. Right, next question. Have you got a camera?
M Yes, I have.
I And what about you, sir? Have you got a camera?
A No, I haven't. I take photos with my mobile.
I Right. And have you got an MP3 player?
M What's an MP3 player?
A They're for music. They're very small.
M Oh, those things. No, I haven't got one of those.
I And you, sir? Have you got an MP3 player?
A Yes, I have.
I Have you got a radio?
A No, I haven't. I listen to the radio on my mobile.
I And you, madam?
M Yes, I have.
I Thanks. Right, the last question. Have you got a DVD player?
A Yes, I have. I watch a lot of DVDs.
I And you, madam? Have you got a DVD player?

M   Yes, I have, but it's very old.
I   Right. Well, madam, we've got some very good DVD players at the moment …

ANSWERS 2 children 4 daughter
5 father 6 mother 7 brother 9 sisters
11 grandchildren 12 grandsons
13 granddaughter 15 uncle 16 cousins
18 grandfather 19 grandmother

Alan's → Pam is Alan's aunt. | Martina's → Greg is Martina's husband. | Florence's → Robbie is Florence's brother. | Ben's → Mary is Ben's wife. | Ben and Mary's → Florence is Ben and Mary's granddaughter.

JILL   Luke, come and look at these photos of my family.
LUKE   OK.
J   Right … This is my sister, Pam, and her husband, Nick.
L   Pam's an English teacher, isn't she?
J   Yes, that's right.
L   What about Nick?
J   He's a doctor.
L   Oh, right. How many children have they got?
J   Two. A boy and a girl. Look, here's a photo of them.
L   Hmm. How old are they?
J   Er, Robbie is six and Florence is about ten months old.
L   They're beautiful.
J   Yes, they are. And this is my brother, Greg. He's an engineer.
L   And who's that?
J   That's Greg's wife, Martina. She's from Italy. Oh, and that's their son, Alan.
L   How old is he?
J   Alan – he's nineteen. He's a student at Cambridge University.
L   Really?
J   Yes, he loves it there. And these are my parents. They're retired now.
L   How old are they?
J   Mum's seventy and Dad's seventy-three. And that's Lily, my favourite member of the family.
L   Sorry, where?
J   There.
L   Oh, the cat!
J   Yes, she's beautiful!

1   A   What time is it?
    B   It's one o'clock.

2   A   What's the time, please?
    B   It's about half past seven.

3   A   Excuse me, have you got the time, please?
    B   Yes, it's four fifteen.
    A   Thanks a lot.

A   Thank you for calling Brent Gallery. We're open Mondays to Fridays from 10 a.m. to 6.30 p.m. and on Saturday and Sunday from 10 a.m. to 4.30 p.m. The exhibition now showing is Mexican Art. [end of CD1 ▶ 42] Ticket prices are £9.50 for adults and £6.50 for children. For more information about the exhibition go to our website at www.brentgallery.org.uk.

B   Welcome to the FilmWorld information and booking line. Here are the films showing at this cinema from Friday June the 10th to Thursday June the 16th. *A New Day*, certificate 12, showing at 4.40, 7.00 and 9.20. *The Brothers*, certificate 15, showing at 5.00, 7.15 and 9.30. [end of CD1 ▶ 42] Ticket prices are £11.50 for adults and £8.25 for children under 16. To book tickets please press 1 or go to our website at www.filmworld.co.uk.

JOSH   Mum?
ALISON   Yes, Josh?
J   Can I have some popcorn?
A   Yes, OK. Here's some money.
J   And can I have a Coke?
A   Yes, OK. But hurry up.

LOUISE   Have you got any money, Chris? If not, I've got my credit card.
CHRIS   No, it's OK. I've got some money. … Hi. Can I have two tickets for *The Brothers*, please?
TICKET SELLER   Yes, of course.
C   How much is that?
TS   That's £23, please.
C   Here you are.
TS   Thanks.
L   What time is the film?
TS   It starts at seven fifteen. Here are your tickets. You're in screen 2.
C   Thanks a lot.
TS   You're welcome. Enjoy the film.
L   We've got 20 minutes before the film starts.
C   OK, let's have a drink first.
L   Good idea.
A   Hello. Can I have two tickets for *A New Day*, please? One adult and one child.
TS   Yes, of course.
A   How much are the tickets?
TS   £11.50 for adults and £8.25 for children. So that's £19.75, please.
A   Here you are. What time's the film?
TS   It starts in two minutes. Here are your tickets. You're in screen 1.
A   Thank you very much.
TS   You're welcome. Enjoy the film.
A   Thanks. Bye. … Hurry up, Josh. The film starts in two minutes.
J   OK.

NICK   Pam, where's my suitcase?
PAM   Here it is, behind the sofa.
N   And have you got my keys?
P   No, Nick, of course I haven't. They're on the desk. By the computer.
N   OK, thanks. And where's my mobile?
P   Oh, I don't know. Look, there it is, under my coat. There, on the sofa!
N   Thanks.
ROBBIE   Mum, where are my new shoes?
P   They're under the chair by the window.
R   And where's my bag?
P   Oh, Robbie. It's by the door. Where it always is.
R   Thanks, Mum.
N   Right. Are you ready, Robbie?
R   Yes.
P   Have you got your school books?
R   Yes, they're in my bag. Look.
N   Oh no! Where's my passport?
P   It's on the table by the window. In front of the plant.
N   Oh yes, thanks.
P   Bye, love. See you on Sunday.
N   Bye.
P   Right … hmm … where's the baby?

FREDDIE   Hello, Jeanette!
JEANETTE   Oh, hello … er …
F   Freddie. Freddie Roberts.
J   You don't work in this office, do you?
F   No, I work in the King Street office.
J   Oh … er … yes, of course.
F   Good party, isn't it?
J   Yes, very nice.
F   Er, Jeanette. Do you go out after work? On Fridays, maybe?
J   No, I don't, sorry. I'm always very tired so I just go home.
F   Right. What do you do in the evenings?
J   I have dinner and watch TV.
F   Do you go to the cinema?
J   No, I don't. But I watch a lot of DVDs.
F   Yes, me too. What do you do at the weekends?
J   Well, on Saturday morning I go shopping. And I don't go out on Saturday evening. I stay in and watch TV.
F   Right.
J   And on Sunday afternoon I visit my parents.
F   Oh, OK. Do you go to concerts?
J   Yes, I do. You know, when I have time.
F   Well, um … I've got two tickets for a concert on Sunday evening. Do you want to come with me?
J   Er … thanks, Freddie, but there's a problem – well, 3 problems, actually.
F   Oh?
J   I'm married! And I've got two children!
F   Oh … well, no problem. Oh look, there's Catherine. Er, I've got something I want to ask her. Excuse me.
J   Really!

CD1 ► 55

1 What do you do in the evenings? (x2)
2 Do you go to the cinema? (x2)
3 What do you do at the weekends? (x2)
4 Do you go to concerts? (x2)

CD1 ► 56

1 A Do you go out a lot in the week?
   B Yes, we do.
2 A Do you visit your parents at the weekend?
   B Yes, I do.
3 A Do you go to concerts at the weekend?
   B No, we don't.
4 A Do you go shopping on Saturdays?
   B Yes, I do.
5 A Do your parents go out on Saturday evenings?
   B No, they don't. They stay in and watch TV.

CD1 ► 58

1 I'm 30 today.
2 We've got a new baby daughter.
3 Today is our 40th wedding anniversary.
4 Guess what! We're getting married!
5 … 5, 4, 3, 2, 1 …

CD1 ► 61

1 A What day is it today?
   B It's Wednesday.

2 A What's the date today?
   B It's the fifth of March.

3 A What's the date tomorrow?
   B It's March the sixth.

4 A When's your birthday?
   B It's on June the third.

CD1 ► 62

1 A When do you start your English course?
   B On September the fifth.

2 A When's your birthday, Sam?
   B It's on the thirteenth of December.
   A Oh, that's on Tuesday!

3 A When's Mother's Day?
   B It's on the fourteenth of March.
   A Oh, that's next week.

4 A When do you start your new job?
   B On the second of July.

5 A Excuse me. What's the date today?
   B It's October the thirtieth.
   A Thanks a lot.

6 A When's Matt and Sarah's wedding anniversary?
   B I think it's the first of February.
   A Oh, no! That's today!

VIDEO ► 3 CD1 ► 63

LOUISE Here's your tea.

CHRIS Thanks a lot.
L Chris?
C Yes?
L What's the date today?
C It's the twenty-ninth. Why do you ask?
L It's Sophie's birthday on Thursday.
C Is it?
L Yes, and I haven't got a present for her.
C Oh. Have you got a card?
L Yes, I have.
C Oh, well. That's OK, then.
L But I want to get her a present too. She's one of our best friends.
C OK then. Let's get her a present.
L Right. What shall we get her?
C Oh, I don't know. What about an MP3 player?
L No, I don't think so. I think she's got one.
C OK then. Why don't we get her a book?
L Maybe. But she's got lots of books.
C Hmm. This is difficult, isn't it?
L Yes, it is.
C I know! Let's get her a DVD.
L Yes, that's a good idea. Sophie and Marcus watch a lot of DVDs.
C And I think they've got a new TV.
L OK. Which DVD shall we get?
C Let's get her a film. Then we can watch it first!
L Chris!

CD1 ► 65

JEANETTE Dominic, do you think I'm a happy person in the morning?
DOMINIC Yes, sometimes. Why do you ask?
J It's this questionnaire. 'Are you an early bird or a night owl?'. I'm sometimes happy in the morning, but I don't have a lot of energy … so that's b.
D What are the other questions?
J Here, come and have a look. Question two, well, that's easy. I hardly ever get up before nine at the weekend.
D Yes, that's true.
J The next question is about parties.
D Oh, that's easy. When we go to a party, you never stay to the end.
J Yes, that's true, I always leave early, don't I? OK, question four. Yes, I often watch films late at night.
D But you never see the end!
J Yes, you're right. So that's c.
D What about question five? When do you see friends at the weekend?
J Well, I usually see friends in the afternoon. Right, the last question.
D Ah, this is a good one.
J Yes, I'm always happy to talk to friends when they phone before eight in the morning.
D What? That's not true! I always answer the phone.
J Yes, you answer the phone, then I talk to my friends. So, it's a. Right, what's my score?
D OK, your score is … um …

CD1 ► 68

POLLY Hi, Lorna. How are you?
LORNA I'm fine. But how are you? You're here and your husband's in Chile!
P Oh, I'm fine. And Trevor's back next month. He's got four weeks' holiday.
L So how is he?
P Well, he's very happy there. The job's great and the hotel's very good. And all of the people are nice. But he doesn't like the weather. It's hot and it hardly ever rains.

CD1 ► 69

POLLY Well, he's very happy there. The job's great and the hotel's very good. And all of the people are nice. But he doesn't like the weather. It's hot and it hardly ever rains.
LORNA What does he do in his free time?
P Well, you know Trevor. He doesn't read a lot, but he plays video games, of course!
L Oh right.
P And he loves sport, so he watches a lot of sport on TV. They've also got a cinema there, so he sees a lot of new films.
L Oh, that's good.
P Yes, and he's got a very good camera, so he takes a lot of photos.
L But he's usually very active – does he do any sport?
P Oh, yes. He plays a lot of tennis. In fact, he has tennis lessons every week. And he goes to the gym every day. He says the gym at the hotel's great. And he goes swimming a lot. But he doesn't go running because it's hot in the day!
L What about running in the evening? It isn't hot then.
P No, he can't. He starts work in the evening! He studies the stars, remember?
L Of course! Do you talk to him very often?
P No, the time difference is a problem. But we email every day and he sends me lots of photos. Here's one I got this morning …

CD1 ► 74

1 What does she do?
2 Does she like rock music?
3 What food does she like?
4 Does she like sport?
5 Does she have any animals?
6 What does she do on Saturday evenings?

VIDEO ► 4 CD1 ► 77

CLARE This is a nice place.
PAUL Yes, it is, isn't it? I hear the burgers are very good here.
C Hmm. The salads look good too. Oh, it's difficult to decide … Yes, the chicken salad, I think.

[See exercise 6a p37]
1   What would you like to drink?
2   Would you like anything else?
3   Would you like a dessert?
4   Would you like tea or coffee?

P   No, don't worry, Clare. Let me pay for this.
C   Are you sure?
P   Yes, of course.
C   OK. Here's a tip.

CD1 79

Would you like to order now? | Yes, I'd like the chicken salad, please. | Can I have the cheeseburger and chips, please? | What would you like to drink? | We'd like a bottle of mineral water, please. | Would you like anything else? | Would you like a dessert? | Yes, I'd like the fruit salad, please. | And can I have the apple pie with cream? | Would you like tea or coffee?

CD1 80

CHEF   Morning, Dylan. Good weekend?
DYLAN   Yes, thank you. And you?
C   Yes, thanks. So, what new nationalities have we got in school this week?
D   New nationalities? Er, we've got Japanese, er French and Turkish.
C   OK. Let's write the new breakfast menus.
D   Yes, chef. So what do the Japanese have?
C   Well, they usually have rice and fish and soup, and they drink green tea.
D   Rice ... fish ... soup and ... green tea. OK. And the French?
C   They have a croissant or toast and jam. Oh and they usually have coffee with milk.
D   Croissant ... toast ... jam ... coffee. Well, that's easy. And what about the Turkish students? What do they have for breakfast?
C   Well, they usually have big breakfasts. They have bread, cheese, eggs, olives and tomatoes.
D   Wow! That's a lot! And to drink?
C   They usually drink tea.
D   OK. So that's bread, cheese, eggs, olives, tomatoes and tea.
C   That's right. OK, Dylan, it's time to start cooking.
D   Actually, it's time for my coffee break!

CD1 82

1   English | musician | Russia | nationality
2   cheese | chicken | sandwich | teacher
3   jam | vegetables | engineer | jazz

CD2 2

JASON   Granddad, when were you born?
ALBERT   I was born in 1953.
J   So you were thirteen in ... 1966.
A   Yes, that's right.
J   And where were you on your thirteenth birthday?
A   I was in Liverpool with my parents.

Oh, I remember that birthday party very well. It was 30th July 1966, the day England won the World Cup.
J   Really? Wow!
A   Yes, the match was in the afternoon and my party was in the evening.
J   That's amazing! Where was the party?
A   It was at my parents' house – and in the street!
J   Was it a big party?
A   Yes, it was. All my friends were there and lots of my parents' friends were there too. There was music and food and dancing in the street – it was a very happy evening!
J   It sounds like a great party. Was the food good?
A   Yes, there were lots of sandwiches and chicken and ice cream, and a birthday cake with a big football on it.
J   Were your grandparents there?
A   No, they weren't. They were in London at the World Cup Final!

CD2 4

I was /wəz/ in Liverpool with my parents. | All my friends were /wə/ at the party. | Our house wasn't very big. | My brothers weren't there. | Where was /wəz/ the party? | Where were /wə/ his grandparents? | Were /wə/ his friends there? | Yes, they were. | No, they weren't. | Was /wəz/ the food good? | Yes, it was. | No, it wasn't. | When were /wə/ you born? | I was /wəz/ born in nineteen fifty-three. | Where was /wəz/ Matt born? He was /wəz/ born in Liverpool.

CD2 6

a August 16th   b 1971   c two   d 1986
e twelve   f $2 billion   g 1999

CD2 10

1   My parents study Italian. My parents studied Italian.
2   They finished work at six. They finish work at six.
3   They stayed in on Saturday. They stay in on Saturday.
4   I live in London. I lived in London.
5   My parents work in Germany. My parents worked in Germany.
6   I visit him every week. I visited him every week.

VIDEO 5   CD2 12

1   EMILY   How was your weekend?
TIM   Terrible. I was ill all weekend.
E   Oh, dear. What was wrong?
T   I had a really bad cold.
E   What a shame. Are you OK now?
T   Yes, much better, thanks. And how was your weekend?
E   It was OK. I stayed at home on Saturday.
T   Oh, right. What did you do?
E   I did the washing, checked my emails, watched TV – you know, the usual.

And then on Sunday I went to the cinema.
T   Oh, nice. What did you see?
E   It was called A Day in the Life.
T   Oh, yes. What was it like?
E   It was great. I really enjoyed it.
T   Yeah, I'd like to see that. Oh, we're late for the meeting. Let's go!

2   SIMON   Hi. How are you?
RACHEL   I'm very well, thanks. I went away for the weekend – to Spain!
S   Wow! Where did you go?
R   We went to Madrid. It was wonderful!
S   Oh, great! Who did you go with?
R   My friend, Ingrid.
S   And where did you stay?
R   We stayed with some friends from university.
S   Oh, nice.
R   What about you? How was your weekend?
S   Oh, not very interesting. I worked all Sunday.
R   Really? What did you do?
S   I wrote that report you wanted. It took me 10 hours.
R   You're joking! When did you finish it?
S   At 11 o'clock last night. Here it is.
R   That's great! Thanks, Simon.
S   No problem.
R   OK, let's start this meeting. Where are Emily and Tim?
S   Here they are.
T   Hi there. Sorry we're late. Emily wanted to get a coffee.
E   Tim!

CD2 13

1   TIM   I was ill all weekend.
EMILY   Oh, dear.

2   TIM   I had a really bad cold.
EMILY   What a shame.

3   EMILY   I stayed at home on Saturday.
TIM   Oh, right.

4   EMILY   I went to the cinema.
TIM   Oh, nice.

5   RACHEL   I went away for the weekend – to Spain!
SIMON   Wow!

6   RACHEL   We went to Madrid. It was wonderful!
SIMON   Oh, great!

7   SIMON   I worked all Sunday.
RACHEL   Really?

8   SIMON   It took me 10 hours.
RACHEL   You're joking!

CD2 16

/ɒ/ hot | coffee | shopping | bottle
/əʊ/ old | sofa | mobile | open
/ʌ/ son | wonderful | sometimes | comfortable
/ə/ actor | tomato | computer | director

They didn't like each other at first.
They didn't finish their course.
They didn't have any money.
They didn't get the money for a month.
They didn't have a bank account.

PRESENTER Welcome to Book of the Day. Today we have the writer Wes Clark, talking about his new book, *Planet Google*. First of all, Wes, is it true? Did you really write this book in twelve weeks?

WES Yes, I did. And I enjoyed writing it because Larry Page and Sergey Brin are really interesting people.

P OK – so, let's start at the beginning. Where are they from?

W Well, Larry Page is American but Sergey Brin was born in Russia. His family went to live in the USA in 1979, when Sergey was six. But his mother wasn't very happy about going to the USA.

P Did she want to stay in Russia?

W Yes, she did.

P So did Sergey's parents find work in the USA?

W Yes, they did. Sergey's father got a job at Maryland University. He was a mathematics teacher there.

P And what about Sergey? Did he study mathematics?

W Yes, he did. He studied mathematics and computer science at the same university.

P At the same university as his father?

W Yes, that's right.

P Did Larry go to Maryland University?

W No, he didn't. He went to Michigan State University. His mother and father were computer science teachers there.

P Really? So Larry was at the same university as his parents!

W Yes, that's correct. And Larry's family always had computers in their home. He was the first student in his school to do his homework on a computer.

P Right. And then Page and Brin went to Stanford University, and now, of course, they're both very rich ...

Did Sergey and Larry meet in nineteen ninety-four? | Did they like each other at first? | Did Sergey go to Maryland University? | Did Larry's parents teach mathematics? | Did Sergey study computer science? | Yes, he did. | No, he didn't. | Did Sergey and Larry launch Google in nineteen ninety-nine? | Yes, they did. | No, they didn't.

1 I can't find my mobile.
2 You can use my phone if you want.
3 A lot of people can't understand it.
4 You can buy 3D TVs online.
5 I can't turn off the TV!
6 Can you download TV programmes?

You can watch TV programmes online. | You can use my phone if you want. | I can't find my mobile. | A lot of people can't understand it. | You could only get three channels. | You couldn't record TV programmes. | Can you watch TV online? | Yes, you can. | No, you can't. | Could you record programmes in nineteen seventy-four? | Yes, you could. | No, you couldn't.

ANSWERS 2 could 3 could 4 could
5 couldn't 6 could 7 couldn't 8 can't
9 can 10 can 11 can't

damage, damaged | sail, sailed | die, died |
receive, received | crash, crashed |
save, saved | buy, bought | lose, lost |
find, found | put, put | say, said | tell, told

ANNOUNCER It's one o'clock and here's George Lucan with the news.

NEWSREADER Over sixty people are in hospital after a train crash in Scotland this morning. The train was on its way to London but crashed only ten minutes after it left Edinburgh.
Fifty-three people died in storms in Florida last night. The storms damaged hundreds of homes and many people are without water and electricity.
Bill and Nancy Potter, who want to be the first eighty-year-old couple to sail round the world, are missing off the coast of Australia. Their family and friends became worried when the couple didn't arrive in Sydney last weekend as planned. Helicopters are now looking for the couple and their boat.
And finally, supermarket manager Joe Hall won over thirteen million pounds in last night's lottery – thanks to his dog! Joe told reporters today that his dog, Max, chose the numbers!

A That's the news this Thursday lunchtime. And now over to Jan Adams for the travel news.

1 PAUL I really enjoyed that burger.
  CLARE Yeah, the salad was good too.
P By the way, did you read about the winner of this week's lottery?
C No. How much did he win?
P Over 13 million pounds.
C Really?
P Yeah, and guess what? His dog chose the numbers for him!

C You're joking! How?
P He wrote 50 numbers on envelopes, put biscuits in them and put them around the house.
C Right.
P And then he used the numbers of the first six envelopes that the dog found. And now he's a millionaire!
C That's amazing!

2 WAYNE Did you hear about that train crash?
  ALISON No, where was it?
W Somewhere near Edinburgh.
A Oh, dear.
W Yes. Over sixty people are in hospital.
A Oh no, that's terrible.
W Yes, I know.
JOSH Mum, Dad, can we talk about the holiday now?
W Yes, OK. Let's have a look ...

3 TIM Here's your coffee.
  EMILY Thanks a lot.
T You have family in the USA, don't you?
E Yes, why?
T Did you hear about the storms in Florida?
E Yes, isn't it awful? I saw it on the news this morning.
T Is your family OK?
E Yes, they're fine. They don't live in Florida. They live near Washington.
T Oh, right. Oh, we're late for a meeting *again*!
E Come on, let's go.

4 CHRIS Did you read about the eighty-year-old couple and their boat?
  LOUISE No, what happened?
C Their boat was damaged in a storm and they were missing for two days.
L Oh, dear. Are they OK?
C Yes. A helicopter found them yesterday off the coast of Australia.
L Oh, that's good.
C Maybe we can sail around the world when we're eighty.
L You're joking, I hope.
C Yes, of course.

Did you hear about that train crash? | No, where was it? | Did you read about the eighty-year-old couple and their boat? | No, what happened? | Oh, that's good. | Oh no, that's terrible. | Yes, isn't it awful? | Oh, dear. Are they OK? | Really? | You're joking!

Tonight's programme looks at the work of Shigeru Miyamoto, the world-famous video game designer. Shigeru was born in Kyoto, Japan, on November 16th 1952. He studied art at Kanazawa College of Art from 1970 to 1975. Between 1998 and 2010 he won awards for his work in the USA, the UK, France and Spain. But Shigeru lives a very

ordinary life. He's married with two children and he usually goes to work by bike. In his free time he plays the guitar and he writes music. He once said, "They say video games are bad for you. But that's what they said about rock 'n' roll." Shigeru designed the first Mario Brothers game in 1983 and he says Mario is his favourite video game character. Shigeru was the first video game designer to tell a story in his video games.

All Mario Brothers video games have a hero, a princess and a villain …

CD2 31

Listening Test (See Teacher's Book)

Phonemic Symbols

Vowel sounds

/ə/	/æ/	/ʊ/	/ɒ/	/ɪ/	/i/	/e/	/ʌ/
father ago	apple cat	book could	on got	in swim	happy easy	bed any	cup under

/ɜː/	/ɑː/	/uː/	/ɔː/	/iː/			
her shirt	arm car	blue too	born walk	eat meet			

/eə/	/ɪə/	/ʊə/	/ɔɪ/	/aɪ/	/eɪ/	/əʊ/	/aʊ/
chair where	near here	tour mature	boy noisy	nine eye	eight day	go over	out brown

Consonant sounds

/p/	/b/	/f/	/v/	/t/	/d/	/k/	/g/
park soup	be rob	face laugh	very live	time white	dog red	cold look	girl bag

/θ/	/ð/	/tʃ/	/dʒ/	/s/	/z/	/ʃ/	/ʒ/
think both	mother the	chips teach	job page	see rice	zoo days	shoe action	television

/m/	/n/	/ŋ/	/h/	/l/	/r/	/w/	/j/
me name	now rain	sing think	hot hand	late hello	marry write	we white	you yes

Irregular Verb List

infinitive	Past Simple	past participle	infinitive	Past Simple	past participle
be	was/were	been	leave	left	left
become	became	become	lose	lost	lost
begin	began	begun	make	made	made
break	broke	broken	meet	met	met
bring	brought /brɔːt/	brought /brɔːt/	pay	paid	paid
buy	bought /bɔːt/	bought /bɔːt/	put	put	put
can	could	been able	read	read /red/	read /red/
catch	caught /kɔːt/	caught /kɔːt/	ride	rode	ridden
choose	chose	chosen	run	ran	run
come	came	come	say	said /sed/	said /sed/
cost	cost	cost	see	saw /sɔː/	seen
cut	cut	cut	sell	sold	sold
do	did	done /dʌn/	send	sent	sent
drink	drank	drunk	sing	sang	sung
drive	drove	driven	sit	sat	sat
eat	ate	eaten	sleep	slept	slept
fall	fell	fallen	speak	spoke	spoken
feel	felt	felt	spell	spelled/spelt	spelled/spelt
find	found	found	spend	spent	spent
fly	flew /fluː/	flown /fləʊn/	stand	stood	stood
forget	forgot	forgotten	swim	swam	swum
get	got	got (US: gotten)	take	took	taken
give	gave	given	teach	taught /tɔːt/	taught /tɔːt/
go	went	been/gone	tell	told	told
have	had	had	think	thought /θɔːt/	thought /θɔːt/
hear	heard /hɜːd/	heard /hɜːd/	understand	understood	understood
hold	held	held	wear	worn	worn
know	knew /njuː/	known /nəʊn/	win	won	won
learn	learned/learnt	learned/learnt	write	wrote	written

Self-study DVD-ROM Instructions

What's on the Self-study DVD-ROM?

- over 300 exercises to practise all language areas
- a Review Video for each unit which appears only on the Self-study DVD-ROM
- *My Tests* and *My Progress* sections
- an interactive Phonemic Symbols chart
- an e-Portfolio with *Grammar Reference*, *Word List* and *Word Cards* practice tool, plus a *My Work* section where you can build a digital portfolio of your work
- the main audio recordings from the Student's Book

Use the navigation bar to go to different areas of the DVD-ROM.

Choose a unit.

Create vocabulary and grammar tests for language in the Student's Book.

Practise the new language from each lesson.

Listen and practise new language. You can also record your own pronunciation.

Watch the Review Video and do the activities.

Listen to the main recordings from the Student's Book and read the scripts.

Go to the home screen.

Get help on using the Self-study DVD-ROM.

Go to Cambridge Dictionaries Online.

Look at the Phonemic Symbols chart and practise the pronunciation of vowel and consonant sounds.

Check *My Progress* to see your scores for completed activities.

Explore the e-Portfolio.